The Guilt of God?

The Guilt of God?

Discovering the Real Meaning of Life in the Kiss of the Divine

David J. Mathews

TATE PUBLISHING
AND ENTERPRISES, LLC

Published by Tate Publishing & Enterprises, LLC
127 E. Trade Center Terrace | Mustang, Oklahoma 73064 USA
1.888.361.9473 | www.tatepublishing.com

Tate Publishing is committed to excellence in the publishing industry. The company reflects the philosophy established by the founders, based on Psalm 68:11,
"The Lord gave the word and great was the company of those who published it."

Cover design by Joseph Emnace
Interior design by Jomel Pepito

Published in the United States of America

ISBN: 978-1-63063-314-1
1. Religion / Christian Life / Inspirational
2. Religion / Christian Theology / General
13.12.13

A Letter of Dedication

Mom and Dad,

I miss you both terribly today. I know you are having a great day, doing whatever dead-yet-alive people do every day. Do you ever think about your days on the earth up there? Do you two talk about us, your children, very often? Do you have pictures of us to show others? Is the house you live up there in like the house in Beaumont? Are there pictures of the grandkids everywhere? Dad, do you know about Maddy, Scottie, Lily, and Mireya? Mom got to meet them and hold them and kiss them.

And how is Josiah? Does he have floppy black hair that's always in his eyes? Do they have T-ball there? And do you get to yell at the umpires? Dad, do you get to make Josiah pancakes with sausage?

And do I ask a lot of questions, or what?

Who do you eat with, and what do you eat, or do you eat? Dad, did you know the Astros finally made the World Series, and that Richard got his younger brother a ticket? Even Weldon got to go with us. Dad, you would have loved being there. There was so much emotion in that stadium. I really thought of you as I walked into the stadium that night. And wouldn't you know it, Dad, the Astros did not disappoint. They played their hearts out, yet barely lost in extra innings, just as we all know they should.

I write this to share a few thoughts with you. There is no way that you, Mom and Dad, will ever totally understand what you did for me and really for many others. Your comeback story has been shared often. What you two did—forgiving each other and loving once again—I cannot adequately explain the impact of that on my life. I just want to say thank you.

Your love for each other not only *saved* my life, but it also *shaped* my life. I was one messed-up, confused kid, not caring if I lived or not, but really caring. I dedicate this book to you, for without you and your love for one another, I truly would be nothing.

I also want to thank you for loving Debbie the way you did. She really is a great wife and mom and Nonni. So knowing you approve, I dedicate this book to her as well. She is so loyal and devoted to me. Without her, I would never have finished the first chapter of this book.

Hug each other for me, and please tell Josiah how wonderful his parents are, and how his entire family misses him.

Thanks, Mom and Dad, for that one night, and one kiss, and those three words—*I love you.*

Acknowledgments

When I was fourteen, my parents moved to Houston and put me in a school of three thousand students, none of whom I knew. It was in this dismal setting that I met one who would profoundly change the course of my life. Though I was a believer in God, I was not a follower of Jesus. Weldon Howard taught me by word and his life that Jesus was real, and that life was worth living. How could I ever thank him enough?

Weldon and I had a senior English teacher who was at least eighty years old, or so we thought. She could barely see, called no one by his right name, and usually had no idea what day of the week it was. Strangely, though, she was an excellent teacher. She understood the art of writing, and without knowing, it encouraged me to pursue writing.

I am sorry I cannot remember her name. I do remember one day she asked the class if anyone had a map of Mexico on them. Not surprisingly no one had one, and I, of course, responded in my sarcastic way, "I am so sorry. I usually carry a map of Mexico on me; I left it at home today." The sad thing is I think she believed me.

The next day, without warning, she asked if anyone had a knife on them. Seventeen of us (all guys) stood up and began reaching in our pockets. This made her very happy, the reasons for which we had no idea. So I want to thank her, for she encouraged me. And I want to acknowledge others as well, though none are quite as quirky as my old English teacher.

A big thanks goes out to Albert Lemons and his precious wife, Patsy. Albert is a modern-day Elijah. He is my mentor, friend, adviser, encourager, and teacher. He prays for me constantly. His insight into Scripture and thus the heart and mind of God inspire me. Though now in his seventies, none surpass his enthusiasm and energy to serve God. He and Patsy have taught thousands about prayer and faith.

My friend Jim Couch was such an inspiration during the entire process of trying to get published. Meeting weekly with him on Thursday mornings helped me not give up the dream. He loved the first draft of the book and would not leave me alone until this was published. Everyone needs a Jim Couch in his life.

I also want to acknowledge the rest of our Thursday-morning group: Gary Hunter, Lyle Sinkey, Tony Brady, and Greg Clark. They too were encouraging and very honest. When I presented the idea that I believed that God has never done anything that did not concern humans, I was not only wrong, some claimed, but also perhaps somewhat arrogant, flaky, and a tad crazy. Everyone needs guys like this in their life, for at least an hour or so. I love these guys.

Mary Hollingsworth of Creative Enterprises was the first editor who worked through the manuscript and gave me invaluable advice in every area of writing a book. Thanks, Mary. You are not only a great friend but also a professional in all your work. I agree to every suggestion she made, simply because she was right, and I trusted her. The same goes for the entire Tate Publishing family. They all have been extremely kind, patient, and professional.

Curt Baker, a retired English professor, was one of the last to edit the book. He found mistakes all the rest of us had missed, and I believe he would find more if time permitted. He and his wife, Judy, have been special to Debbie and me in too many ways to count. I hope you both know what you mean to us.

And, of course, I want to thank my family, who remain such a source of strength to me. Unknowingly, they provided much of the initial material and inspiration of the book. My sister Ann and brother Richard were there the night Mom kissed Dad again. Their love and support over the years for their younger brother—me—have never wavered. Thank you, both.

God has blessed me with a wonderful wife, four incredible children, and sons- and daughters-in-law who love our children. So to Adam and Rebekka, Sara and Jason, Kelly and Joel, and Chuck and Shelly, I love you greatly.

And to Madalyn, Lillian, Scotland, and Mireya, well, all I can say is that what they say about the greatness of grandchildren is simply not true—it is better than that and is unexplainable. You know that love is there, but it is difficult to describe. When they give Papa and Nonni a kiss, it really is experiencing the divine kiss. And this I think is what it is all about.

Contents

Part II The High Stakes of Being Human

Introduction

PART ONE–THE HIGH STAKES OF BEING GOD

Today is December 14, 2012. It will live in infamy. Today, twenty children and six adults were gunned down by one who was a human, who is now also dead. The questions of why will never be adequately answered. Today, one who was once a baby, who others once thought was so cute and beautiful, was *evil*, *wicked*, and *cruel*. And those words fail to convey the depth of his sickness and depravity. Today, many are questioning, not only the laws of the land, but also the very meaning of our existence. Today demands answers and demands them quickly.

> Why did this loving God create those lives six years ago, knowing very well he was going to allow their murder at such a young age? This God has a very strange way of showing his love. Did he regret creating those lives? Is he *nuts*? Or did he just want to inflict the maximum pain and grief on the parents? How can you call this God "loving," who is present at a terrible carnage and does *nothing* to stop it?

These questions, which I read as an anonymous post a few days after the carnage in Connecticut, evidently represent millions of humans trying to make *sense* of the *nonsense*. Not all of these are from hedonistic heathens; many come from religious people of all types. There is no monopoly, by any group, on the tough questions concerning the apparent contradictions of the Supreme Being, all-powerful and all-loving, doing nothing to prevent such atrocities.

And as we all know, this confusion is not just about December 14, 2012. It is about every single day of human history that is filled with horror, hunger, disaster, and disease.

I want to believe in God. Then again, there are times when I absolutely do not believe in the god that I hear presented by those who profess faith in God. One example suffices: on October 17, 1989, a woman was in her car on a bridge during the San Francisco earthquake. As she and her car came crashing down, she cried out to God to save her. According to her, God did indeed save her. She did not die. As her story of God's deliverance echoed throughout the religious broadcasting circles, others chimed in about their great and caring God leading rescuers to find some trapped in debris, some still alive days after the earthquake. "Isn't God great?" many asked.

For the record, I do believe that God is great. In fact, he is greater than great. But I have some problems concerning a god who is praised for leading rescuers to find badly burned and crippled bodies of children after an earthquake, barely alive. Yet apparently he either did not have enough power or did not care enough to *prevent* the earthquake in the first place. Could not a god who saved a woman from certain death whose car plummeted one hundred feet, not also save the sixty-three others who died, or the 3,757 who were injured? Or was she just more special to God than all the others?

Back to December 14, 2012. I simply must ask this question: Did God know all that would happen in that quiet Connecticut town before it all went down? Did he know when and how Adam Lanza prepared for his acts? My previously held concept of God assumed that he did. It also assumed that, with a snap of his finger, God could have prevented the entire fiasco. If these assumptions are correct, then without question God, who could have prevented the mass destruction as easily as I am typing these words, simply did not desire to stop it.

However, that was my previously held concept. Now I do not assume that God knew every detail of yet-to-happen events. God appeared to come to knowledge of Abraham's love for him when Abraham took back the knife (see Genesis 22: 10-12, "Now I know…"). And if somehow he could and did know (as he somehow knew that Peter would deny Jesus and Judas would betray Jesus), I am now not convinced that he could have prevented it, and at the same moment kept Adam Lanza as a free-will human being. But enough of that now. We will discuss all of that in detail later.

I want to believe in God. I *do* believe in God. But if I am to give all of myself to another Being (God), then I want to be convinced that this Being is actually real, and that he is truly a loving and caring God. Some descriptions of this Being do not warm this old heart to even the *idea* of the Being. Faith is not about hoping that God might exist, and hoping that perhaps he does love me. Faith is being certain of what we hope for, and that he rewards those who seek him (see Hebrews 11). Paul states that we have a reason for the hope we have (1 Peter 3:15 NIV).

I readily admit that God, being the infinite One, cannot be totally understood by finite beings such as we. But I am convinced that God, being the infinite from which we all have come, should be powerful enough to be able to make his presence known. It must be possible for me, a finite human being, to know that God is and that God cares for me. I do believe the problem of coming to this realization resides in us, and not in him. There is no weakness with the true God.

Paul, who had quite a journey in his "True God" finding, made a claim that appears many believers have never truly believed.

> For who knows a person's thoughts except their own spirit within them? In the same way no one knows the thoughts of God except the Spirit of God. What we have received is not the spirit of the world, but the Spirit who is from God, so that we may understand what God has freely given us.
>
> 2 Corinthians 2:11-12 (NIV)

The claims in this passage are shocking to many. Ordinary humans can know the thoughts of God! Only the Spirit of God knows God's thoughts, and Paul is claiming that believers now have the Spirit of God, and thus may come to understand what God has freely given us.

God deeply desires to be spoken of in a right way (Job 42:7 NIV). Humans, being human, often speak of him in wrong ways. When God's reputation is slandered, at the very least he is frustrated, and at the most his anger is aroused. Why? Because when God is misrepresented, many people decide, "If that is God, then forget it." Though we cannot totally understand God, he desires that we understand enough of him to know him.

I made a comment in a class recently that if God can save one more person from hell and does not, then I will not give my heart to that god. I also stated that if God does not do all he can do to save us, *all* he can do, then I would choose not to love him. The reasons for such apparently slanderous statements are discussed fully in this book. Please do not judge me and those convictions just yet.

Fortunately, I made it out of the class alive and somehow kept my job as the minister. But God has the right to do whatever he pleases, one reasoned. Yes, of course he does, I answered. And the Bible says that what he desires is that every human be saved, that no one be lost (1 Timothy 2:4, 2 Peter 3:9 NIV). Since he does not want any to be lost, if he *could* save them, then he indeed will.

If he can, but simply chooses not to save them, then I am really conflicted about this god.

Recently, I heard a well-known and deeply respected preacher state confidently that God will not save everyone because he never intended to. If he intended to save everyone, the speaker continued, then He most certainly would. Many Christians apparently believe this, though certainly not every believer buys that theory. I am a believer, but I cannot and will not accept that view of God, for many reasons. God desires to save everyone; if every human is not saved, then the only conclusion is that God cannot save everyone. And his heart breaks.

A friend of mine praised God for giving her a parking space at Wal-Mart close to the entrance. She just really needed that, she said. Though, of course, God could have somehow used his power to free up a parking space, I must admit that the friend's comment irked me. A few weeks earlier our grandson died, in spite of repeated pleas with God to save him. So God responds because someone does not want to walk a few extra feet in the Wal-Mart parking lot, but he turns a deaf ear to two pleading parents, four desperate grandparents, and a host of other family and friends to save their son? This *god* does not thrill me. Just being honest here.

I, for one, have great difficulty in serving a god who appears more interested in securing a parking space for someone than preventing, literally, millions of humans he created to suffer from such things as school shootings, earthquakes, abuse, abandonment, and hunger, among a myriad other horrors of this life.

No, this is *not* the God I love. We must speak of him in a right way. While we can never get to the top of this mountain on this earth (of knowing God fully and completely), there simply must be a way for us to know that God is and that God cares. (See again 1 Corinthians 2:10-11.) My conviction is that we might have made it more difficult than it actually is.

This book proposes that God knows that he is ultimately responsible for the mess of this world, because he created this world. He feels the responsibility to do whatever he can do to fix the problem. Though God cannot be charged with sin and is not to be blamed for our sins, he is to be blamed for our being here and for our having the free choice to sin. Thus, if you were God, might you feel a bit guilty for the horrors of this world? Though none of us can totally understand all of it, this I do know: no one else has attempted to solve the problems of this world as God has. He and he alone can get us out of this mess. God knows it and feels the heavy responsibility.

There is indeed high stakes in being God. Knowing and believing that God has done, and will do, whatever it takes to save us has absolutely changed my life. Believing this can and will change your life as well. God is on our side, in spite of the apparent evidence that there are more obstacles and roadblocks than any help from God.

PART TWO–THE HIGH STAKES OF BEING HUMAN

Today is December 16, 2012. I have just listened to a father of a six-year-old girl killed in the Connecticut disaster. He not only asked the country to pray for all of the parents and relatives of those killed by Adam Lanza, he asked us to remember and pray for the family of the killer. They are hurting also, he reminded us. Once again, we were reminded that good still resides in people. People can be so evil. We all know that. But people also can be so God-like. Incredible stories abound of heroic people doing truly heroic things. And though some of these stories end up as best-selling books or award-winning movies, most of these stories concern what we call ordinary people doing extraordinary things. Every one of us has had first-hand experience with someone who falls into the category of "Are you kidding?"

People I have known prove beyond a doubt that there is something beyond our human existence. The human spirit awes us. And though certainly all of us have been disappointed with humans at times, none can deny the unexplained, incredible human response to crushing defeats, injustices, and failures.

But some thoughts haunt me. Why do so many people accept mediocrity in their lives? Why do so many abandon their dreams and grow bitter and angry as the years roll by? If God exists, and if he truly loves us and cares for us, then why do the majority of believers I know doubt that he truly loves them? Why the struggle to find God and know God, and why does it appear next to impossible to really have a deep and abiding fellowship with God? And though some who are reading this have found him and bask in his love and care, why are the majority of the seven billion on this planet in survival mode?

If you could be as objective as possible as a participant in the drama called living, who would you say is winning the battle for our souls? Is it God or Satan? At least to me, Satan appears to be winning. If the game ends with Satan on the winning side, then the belief that God is the all-powerful, eternal One takes a huge hit. No, Satan cannot be the winner if God exists, and is all-good and all-powerful.

Though there are many unanswered questions concerning God, life, and us, there must be some answers. I believe there are enough answers, and that these can be known by us right now. I disagree with Zophar, one who counseled Job after he lost everything.

> Can you fathom the mysteries of God? Can you probe the limits of the Almighty? They are higher than the heavens above—what can you do? They are deeper than the depths below—what can you know? Their measure is longer than the earth and wider than the sea.
>
> Job 11:7-9 (NIV)

Many appear to accept without question Zophar's conclusion, though perhaps in more subtle ways, that if we cannot understand all things about God, then we cannot know anything about God. We know better, for believing we cannot totally understand God *is* knowing something about God! When we discover some of the answers, exhilaration of living can return. Mediocrity can be smashed to bits. Living the way God intended is possible. God must turn out to be the absolute winner. His creation must also be able to win. There are high stakes in being human. God knows it and believes it. It is time we believe it too.

PART I
THE HIGH STAKES OF BEING GOD

One Night, One Kiss, Three Words

All this came down on us, and we've done nothing to deserve it... Do we deserve torture... or lockup in a black hole?... No, you decided to make us martyrs...

Get up, God! Are you going to sleep all day? Wake up! Don't you care what happens to us? Why do you bury your face in the pillow? Why pretend things are just fine with us? And here we are—flat on our faces in the dirt, held down with a boot on our necks. Get up and come to our rescue. If you love us so much, *Help us!*

Psalm 44 (MSG, selected verses)

My parents had the perfect marriage. Often I bragged to my friends at school about it, taking pride in their love for one another. But one night in the '60s changed that thinking; in fact, it changed everything.

It was 1963. The Dodgers won the World Series over the hated Yankees, sweeping them in four straight. My Texas Longhorns were 11-0, beating Roger Staubach and Navy in the Cotton Bowl, and were crowned national champions. Life was pretty good for a thirteen-year-old living in Texas.

Then that fateful night arrived. The day innocence was shattered—the moment in history when I discovered fairy tales were exactly that—fairy tales. It was the night an appalling truth crashed upon me: Mom and Dad did not have a perfect marriage. Mom and Dad hated each other.

I do not recall what they fought about that night, but I remember enough to know that awful feeling deep inside of me, gnawing away any sense of stability. Their fighting intensified as the weeks and months rolled by. Every weekend was the same—yelling, cursing, hate-filled words slung back and forth.

Finally, Dad moved out.

Writing those words forty-seven years later still stings. At times I wonder if parents really comprehend the negative impact those three words have on a child's thinking: *Why? Why the hate? Why does Dad have to leave? Why can't they love each other the way I love them both? Why can't they forgive, and start all over? Why doesn't God do something about it? Why can't my daddy live with us? And why doesn't the hurt go away?*

Parents seem to forget the hurt they unintentionally inflict on their kids. But sometimes, parents remember.

It was a Sunday morning. We had not heard from Dad in weeks. I actually thought I might never see him again. The phone rang. It was Dad. "You guys want to play golf?" What a dumb question!

Dad, don't you realize that all I want to do is to be with you? I miss you. Since you moved out, life has taken a tumble. I have pimples, I'm fat, and all the girls laugh at me. I have only one friend in the world, and he's almost as weird as I am. I don't care about anything, yet I do care. I'll do anything with you. Sure, Dad, we'll play golf with you.

So we played, but we hardly talked. Darkness came much too soon, and as much as I hated it, we headed home. "Thanks for the golf, Dad. Do you have to go so soon? Please stay a few minutes.

Mom is not home yet. You can leave when she gets here. Please, Dad."

So he stayed. We drank iced tea. We mostly sat, dreading the coming separation. And then Mom walked through the door.

To fully grasp the impact of that night, a few painful facts need to be revealed. They had been living apart for a few months, but they had been emotionally separated much longer. They had not kissed, hugged, held hands, or slept in the same bed for years. They had not, at least to my knowledge, used the word *love* to each other in ages.

Whether she knew it or not, Mom was about to give my sister, brother, and me the greatest gift imaginable.

It was around 10 p.m. when she opened that door and walked in. Dad began to get up to leave, but she stopped him. "Tom, you can stay as long as you want. I'm tired and going to bed." My sister and brother were sitting there with us. So Mom made the rounds to say good night.

"Good night, Ann. I love you." She then kissed my sister on the cheek.

"Good night, Richard. I love you." She kissed my brother on the cheek.

"Good night, David. I love you." And she kissed me on the cheek.

She paused. We sensed that she was not yet finished with the good nights. But there was only one other person in the room. He was sitting in a big chair to my left. And though it has been nearly fifty years since that night, I see his face so vividly, and I hear her words so clearly.

She walked over to Dad. With compassion, love, and tenderness such as I had never seen before, she kissed her husband, our daddy, on the cheek.

"And I love you, too, Tom."

She left the room. Dad finally said good night and left to go back to his apartment. No one mentioned the miracle we just experienced. Stunned is too mild a word to describe the feelings.

The next day, as I was sitting alone in the den, the doorbell rang. As I opened the door, there was Dad holding a couple of boxes with clothes slung over his shoulder. "Can you help me move my stuff into the house?"

So that's how my daddy came home to stay. For the next twenty-seven years, he and Mom held hands, kissed, hugged, and, yes, slept in the same bed. They loved each other with the love of the ages.

Why? What happened? For twenty years, I asked that question to no one in particular. One day I was working on a sermon about comebacks. I always loved those stories where the underdog looks defeated and then makes a miraculous recovery, when no one believes winning is a possibility. And it hit me: the greatest comeback I have ever witnessed was the night Mom kissed Dad again. But I did not know the answer to that big "Why?" question.

So I called Mom and read the story I had written concerning that one night. I asked her if it was true, or had I imagined it? "If it is true," I continued, "what happened, Mom? Why did you do that?"

Mom could hardly respond. No one in the family had ever said a word about that night. Tears flowed. Alzheimer's disease was beginning to ravage Dad's mind, which added more emotion upon her hearing the story.

Finally Mom spoke, saying, "First, every word of the story is true. You remembered it exactly as it happened. But I am surprised that you do not know why we got back together. I thought it was obvious. You three kids were a mess when Dad moved out. I simply could not bear to see all of you in such pain. So I decided to love your father again, and he decided to accept that love."

So there you have it: they decided to love each other again.

Years after the night of the kiss, Mom was diagnosed with breast cancer. I arrived at the hospital after traveling all day. As I walked into her room, I found Dad sitting in a big chair to my left. He was holding his bride's hand and gently stroking her hair and forehead.

And my mind raced back to that fateful night, when love was reborn. One night, one kiss, three words.

To The Victor Goes...

> When the perishable has been clothed with the imperishable, and the mortal with immortality, then the saying that is written will come true: "Death has been swallowed up in victory."
>
> 1 Corinthians 15:54 (NIV)

Vietnam. Drugs. Women who were not his wife. Woodstock. Motorcycles and Hell's Angels in black, leather pants and jackets. Long, greasy hair; a beard rarely combed, with food scattered throughout. Unwashed bandana around his head. A fifty-three-year-old face looking sixty-five.

Spiritually dead by his admission. Renounced God, "if there is a God," years ago. Living for self and proud of it. "Born to be Wild" was his favorite song.

Yet somehow that *loser* changed my life for good and for God, because someone loved him and refused to give up on him.

She was nearly ninety, but didn't look a day over eighty-five. Impeccably dressed, every hair in place. A beautiful, older woman. I kidded my wife, "If you look that good when you're sixty, I'd be proud."

She laughed, "If you looked that good now, I would be proud too."

His name was Victor. Her name was Julia. She, of course, was his mama. And moms rarely give up on their kids.

"David, would you pray for my youngest son, Victor? He found out he has cancer, and there's nothing they can do for him."

I did not know that Julia had another son. "Well, Victor is different from our other son. He used to love God, but Vietnam changed everything. When he came back, he was different. Drugs became his god. He renounced God years ago."

I asked what hospital he was in, and her response surprised me.

"Oh, you can't go see him. He hates preachers. He would probably have you thrown out of his room."

I responded that it could not hurt to try to see him. The worst that could happen, I reasoned, would be a few unkind words. And he would not have to know that I was a preacher. I admit that one of my goals as I dress every morning is to not come close to looking like a preacher.

So off I went to see Victor. Upon entering his room, he was as I expected, except worse. Not only did he look like a reprobate, he resembled a dying heathen.

"And who are you?" he bellowed as I entered his room. Just a friend of your mother's. "You must be a preacher. And I have no use for preachers. So you can just leave the same way you came in."

Thus started our relationship—Victor and me.

Being stubborn can occasionally be a good thing. That was one of those times. "I came all this way to see you, so I am not leaving. And by the way, who's your friend?"

His friend actually looked worse than Victor. He was wearing a Hell's Angels leather jacket. His beard was to his navel, and some teeth were missing, about thirty-one or -two of them.

"That's Harold. He is my best friend, and he will hurt you if you don't leave now. If you don't believe me, just ask the convicts he used to whip."

I quickly re-evaluated the "worst thing that could happen to me" scenario. But when I saw the wink of my newfound, toothless friend, Harold, courage returned with vigor.

"Victor, do you mind if we have a prayer before I leave?"

This technique, learned years ago, had never failed in twenty years of visiting in hospitals. Believer and unbeliever alike would always answer in the positive, until Victor.

"Yes, I mind. I mind very much. You will not pray for me. I forbid it! Now get out of here. I knew my mother sent you."

I sensed he was not kidding. His face, already a reddish tint, was becoming redder. Veins, infiltrated by tubes, seemed to be protruding beyond the safe zone. Harold simply shrugged, as if he was warning me to leave.

"All right," I stammered, "I'm leaving. But when I step out that door, I *am* going to pray for you. You cannot stop me."

"Oh, yeah?" he shouted.

"Yeah!" I shouted louder. Temporarily, I thought I was back in third grade, arguing with me best friend, Roger. I concluded with a confident, "See you next week, Victor."

As I stepped out into the hallway, the temptation hit me to pray out loud—really loud: "Lord, please be with the ugliest and rudest man I have ever met, Victor." But, being the saint I am, I simply prayed that prayer silently.

As the months passed, Victor was in and out of the hospital. As my visits continued, Victor held fast. Every visit was the same. ESPN was always on in his room. We would talk about the Detroit Tigers, Lions, Pistons, and Red Wings. Victor was getting thinner; the chemo was not working. Death inched closer. The visits would end the same. "Victor, may I pray with you?"

He would shout an obscenity, say "Absolutely not," and Harold would shrug. I would walk out the room and pray for him in the hallway silently.

One Friday morning the phone rang. It was Julia, in tears. Victor had lapsed into a coma; the end was near. Could we please come to the hospital?

While driving to see him, guilt overwhelmed me. I had not visited with Victor in a while. I had not exactly given up on him, but I had not persevered much with him either. It was too late to talk with him once more, and I had never prayed with him.

Julia had told me that the doctors said he had a few hours to live at the most. He could die at any moment, and he would never awaken. I am glad to report that doctors are sometimes wrong.

As we walked to his room, Julia came running out to meet us. She was excited. "Victor woke up a few minutes ago. He wants to talk with you."

So here I am, I thought, *holding the hands of a dying Vietnam vet, who is angry with God, thinking that God long ago stopped loving him.* For a minute or so, I stood speechless, not knowing what to say. Finally, words tumbled out.

"Victor, this is David. Can you hear me?"

"Yes," he mumbled.

"Victor, I love you. I hope you know that."

"Yes," he mumbled.

"Victor, do you know that God loves you too?"

Suddenly, he spoke clearly, "God could not love me, David. If you knew all that I have done, you would agree with me."

I told him that I did know what he had done, because his mother had told me. He winced, acting embarrassed that those sharing his last moments on earth knew what a scoundrel he had been. I also shared with him the thief on the cross story, the condemned man who uttered simple words before dying: "Lord, remember me when you come into your kingdom."

Victor knew that story. Before Vietnam he had studied for the ministry. He had preached, taught Bible classes, and shared Jesus with others. And I thought I knew the story of the thief on the cross as well. But I was wrong; I did not know that story until that day. Victor taught it to me.

"How could God forgive me? I have turned my back on him. I have been so sinful, so bitter."

"I don't know, Victor, how He could love you. And I don't know how He could love me. But this I know, Victor. He has never stopped loving you. The cross proves that." I mumbled some other things, thinking my words were a bit *preachery*. I would have given me a D if I were grading my response to a dying man.

After awkward moments of silence, Victor spoke. "David," he began, "would you pray with me? You think you could ask God to forgive me?"

I do not know much about your theology. There are times when I do not know much about mine. But at that moment I believed this about God and sin: God knew Victor's heart, and he knew Victor's sin. The forgiveness God gave to Victor had nothing to do with my prayer for him. The forgiveness had everything to do with the blood of Jesus, and thus the love of God. All Victor needed to do was to ask for it and accept it.

So I finally got to pray with Victor, not to beg God to forgive him, but to thank God for forgiving him. After the prayer, I leaned over and gave this former reprobate a tender kiss on his tear-streaked cheek. I knew the power of a well-timed kiss. And I was privileged, for the first time, to see Victor cry.

An hour later, he died. In reality, Victor was set free. And I was reminded of a familiar passage, which has Victor's name all over it:

"Death has been swallowed up in victory" (1 Corinthians 15:54, NIV).

The God of the Dirt

> These things are not strange, Small One, though they are beyond our senses.[1]
>
> —C.S. Lewis

When he was three, my son Adam and I went out to the backyard. Past our small patio was a section of ground that was mostly dirt. Though I had shed much blood and sweat, grass refused to grow. No amount of fertilizer, knowledge, experimentation, loads of dirt, seed, sods of grass, pleading, begging, or praying could get the grass to grow.

So my son decided to sit in the dirt. I decided to sit with him.

"Adam, let's talk. You can start, I will listen. Whatever you want to talk about." Even though I had only been a father for these three years, I had read enough to know how to be a great dad—spend time with your children.

So we sat in the dirt together. Life seems to always go back to the dirt.

"So Adam, what do you want to talk about? Superman, Santa Claus, the Smurfs?" (It was 1981.)

"God." His response was simple and electrifying. My son wanted to talk about God! I could write this in my book someday, and it would look good on the resume. Preachers who have three-year-old sons who do not like God have trouble getting good jobs.

"Okay, God it is. Let's talk about God. What do you want to say about God?"

The sun broke through the clouds at that exact moment. A rainbow suddenly appeared. Life was good, almost too good. My son and I were in the backyard discussing God. My wife was in the house with our one-year-old daughter, Sara, doing girl stuff. A roast was in the oven, flowers were blooming, and there was no visible dirt in the house. The entire scenario reminded me of the 50's television series 'Leave it to Beaver.' I think June Cleaver was cleaning the house with the dress on that she always wore. Then the Beaver and Wally would come home from school and kiss their mom, thanking her for the snack she had set on the table for them. Ward was about to come home and keep his tie on until bedtime. I have never figured that one out, by the way.

"Dad," he began, "did God plant those flowers over there?"

"Yes, of course he did, son."

"Did he plant the trees and bushes?"

"Yes, he did," *my brilliant God-loving little boy.*

His face somehow grew more serious as he contemplated his next question. A look of confusion engulfed him. "Dad, did God plant this dirt we are sitting on?" In all my years of living, thirty-one at that time, I had never considered whose fault dirt was.

"Why yes," I replied, "God must have planted the dirt also, Adam."

"Why, Daddy? Why so much dirt? You always complain about the dirt here. Why doesn't God just get rid of the dirt?"

I didn't answer him because I couldn't.

But did God plant the dirt? If so, why? And then the big question that has baffled humans for ages: Why doesn't he get rid of the dirt, or at least make the pile smaller? And as we grow older, it appears the amount of dirt multiplies. The dirt piles can become overwhelming.

Why so much dirt, God?

Why did Alex, Greg and Joan's only child, an innocent four-year-old, die suddenly?

Why did Jon and Rachel's healthy, happy ten-year-old scream early one Christmas morning and die in his bed? Why couldn't the doctors discover the reason he died? Perhaps this is being a bit picky, but if he had to go, why on Christmas morning? Jon and Rachel will never again sing "Tis the Season to be Jolly."

Why was Mary sexually abused by her own father from the age of four until her thirteenth birthday, and why were her nightly cries to her loving, all-powerful Father—you—seemingly ignored?

Why did my dad suffer from Alzheimer's disease, along with millions of others? Why didn't you take him home before Mom had to change his diapers?

Of course, I have not even asked about the millions of kids going to bed hungry every night, or the thousands of innocents through the ages being abused, ignored, beaten, or disease infested.

Dare I be so bold, but one more question for you, Father: if you exist, why is it so very difficult at times to believe in you and trust you? Shouldn't it be natural for the created ones to know and trust the Creator?

Do such questions bother you? I hope so, for it means you are thinking. The tendency for many, I believe, is to ignore the questions. It is almost easier. Some say just believe, have a blind faith. Perhaps that works for you. I have tried it, and as for me, I do not want to ignore the questions, for many reasons.

First, God is certainly 'big' enough to handle the questions. As a parent of four children, I usually welcomed their tough questions. Questions meant they were searching for answers.

Any child of mine honestly seeking would be rewarded, not scolded.

Second, there are answers to those questions. When we discover some of the answers, then God's *wowness* increases. Obviously, some questions will remain a mystery on this side of eternity. But as long as I have a few "Aha!" moments with God, I am okay. Occasionally, I need a trip up the mountain of transfiguration. I must hear a voice in some manner that reminds me to "listen to him!" (Matthew 17:5 NIV). Perhaps seeing Moses and/or Elijah would help a little also. The questions, and the answers, and yes the non-answers, help me deal with all the dirt–the dirt of the past, the dirt of the present, and all the dirt surely to come.

Third, the claim of God's existence demands that we have questions and that we never totally "get it." Why? Because if God exists, then he has never *not* existed. He is infinite. He is the first cause of all existing things. He has always been. He came from nothing and depends on nothing else for his existence. I exist, but I have not always existed. I was not around when Babe Ruth hit his sixtieth homerun. There was a time when I was *not.*

If finite humans could totally understand the infinite, always-been God, at least in this fallen world, there could be no God. He would be the invention of the human mind, a concept with human limitations. In other words, it makes sense that humans will not have absolute answers to all the God questions. Yet it also makes sense that we have to have some answers. There is too much dirt not to wash my hands every now and then.

THE ONTOLOGICAL ARGUMENT

St. Anselm, 1033-1109, was the archbishop of Canterbury and the originator of the Ontological Argument for the existence of God. If you find yourself bored some night, google the ontological argument and begin reading. One of two things will occur when you do this. You will make three or four pots of coffee and stay up all night reading, thinking, and eventually screaming that you just can't take it anymore. Or perhaps you will read one or two paragraphs before politely, yet intentionally, ripping every single page into tiny pieces, which would be a bit difficult since you were reading this on your computer. However, there is something about this argument that captivates the searching soul.

The following few paragraphs might be tough for some to wade through without throwing this book down in disgust. I encourage you, of course, since I am writing this to not do that. I promise that the rest of the book is not like this. This is not a theological or a philosophy of religion textbook. Primarily, the concern of this book is to speak right of God. Many in the intellectual community attack believers in God, accusing us of being totally illogical. The reason for this brief discussion on Anselm is to show that believing in something that has no beginning or end is logical; in fact, it is the only possible explanation of our being here.

The rest of the book will attempt to put meat on the bones of this thing that has always been. What does the uncaused cause look like? That which is infinite, as previously noted, cannot be totally understood by those of us who have not always been. But we must be able to understand something about this infinite being, for the infinite first cause is the original source of our "being." If God indeed exists, there is something of God within each of us.

Suffering and pain have long caused many people to question the existence of a personal and loving first cause. Misrepresentations of God, especially in the realm of pain and suffering, have led many to assume there is no first cause at all. The popular Big Bang Theory never deals with the fundamental question: "What is the origin of the stuff that exploded? Did it come from nothing? Or has it always been?" The only answer is the latter. So everyone believes in some kind of infinite source. Some just do not know that yet.

To many people the concept of God is absurd. Not only do they question how something could "always be," they assume an all-powerful being could and would eliminate all pain and suffering. The immensity of suffering in our world (many claim) contradicts a God purported to be all-powerful and all-loving. However, I am convinced that many who have rejected the idea of God have not rejected the true God; they have refused to believe in *a* god. The true God must be spoken of in a right way. We will attempt to do that, though admitting the difficulty of the assignment and the imperfections of this author.

Now back to Mr. Anselm. The cornerstone phrase Anselm was known for, and which is a part of the Ontological Argument, is that God must be thought of as "a being than which nothing greater can be conceived."[2] Anselm is simply stating that one cannot conceive of a being greater than the greatest being! God, whoever or whatever God is, is that being that no other being which we conceive of could surpass.

Anselm argued that God must exist, that he exists necessarily, and that "God possesses a kind of existence that is possessed by no other thing."[3] John Hick also approached God's existence from the "necessary" position. God cannot *not* exist, he wrote[4].

There are two reasons I reference Anselm. First, whether one is a theist, an atheist, or an agnostic, everyone who thinks through this "How did we get here?" question must come to one inevitable conclusion: whatever started this thing called life must be self-existent, depending on nothing for its existence. This is true because if *something* did not always exist, then the first *thing* to exist came from absolutely nothing, which happens to be impossible. *Something* cannot come from *nothing*. Thus, the original *something* must have been in existence forever. No other being possesses the kind of existence as this Supreme Being. In other words, one being must have a kind of existence different than all others, else every being would be dependent on another. *Something* independent had to start this *thing* called "existence."

My wife was adopted as an infant. Recently, we found her birth mother and actually were able to meet her shortly before her death. This experience has changed both of us. Her birth father is dead. We have never even seen a picture of him.

But this we know: Debbie's birth father did indeed exist. No one would deny that fact. The reasoning is simple: we all have to come from something outside ourselves. Someone has to precede us. You probably did not have to read this to know that. But everything in existence cannot possibly come from something else. There has to be one thing that is not dependent on something else for its existence.

This uncaused first cause is not an exclusive Judeo-Christian teaching or dogma. It is simply true. There are no other explanations. There must be something that possesses a different kind of existence that is possessed by no other being. If all in existence is contingent on something else, then that something else is contingent also. No, there simply must be a first cause that has a different kind of existence than all other existing things. This first cause must exist, as John Hick explains, and this first cause must have existence as part of its make-up; existence must come from *within* that being and not without. Thus, that being must exist, its existence is thus "necessary." Humans do not have the quality of always existing within us. We owe our existence to things outside of us, such as parents and grandparents.

Confused yet?

The question is not whether something infinite (that which has no beginning or end) exists. The question is, "What *is* this infinite thing that must exist?" What does it look like? Is that which has always been simply matter and molecules and gases with no personality or emotion? Or must that which has always been contain both personality and emotion? And "it" must be the most powerful thing we could imagine—so powerful that it depends on nothing for its existence, and so powerful that it is the source of all that exists today.

Another reason I allude to this great thinker of the past is his relentless pursuit to understand God more fully, yet realizing he can never totally know the creator and Father of us all: "I do not endeavor, O Lord, to penetrate thy sublimity, for in no wise do I compare my understanding with that; but I long to understand to some degree thy truth, which my heart believes and loves."[5]

While studying the Ontological Argument can be an exercise in futility for many, a longing to understand some degree of truth should be an exercise for all of us. Believing in this God might not only be the logical answer for our being here, it could also be easier than we have made it, and getting to know God does not always have to be so difficult. After all, if this being is the source of all that exists, he must be everywhere (Psalm 139:7–12). And since he is self-existent, he is all-powerful. Thus revealing himself to us in a way in which we can say confidently, "He is and he cares for me" should be no problem for him. I do believe the problem resides in us and not in God. (Again see 1 Corinthians 2:11-12)

Although the preceding can be a bit confusing to all of us at times, remember this: we humans are the only part of creation privileged to be confused. I do not believe dogs and cats discuss such things or read books such as this.

BACK TO THE KISSES

The night Mom kissed Dad not only changed my family's history, it also changed my God history. God came out of theory and into life, or better yet, into my heart. I do not know what my life would be like without that kiss.

The day I kissed Victor and finally got to pray with him changed me also. God seemed to "get" Victor, so Victor finally "got" God. God does not seem to have *give up* in his vocabulary.

We all need similar kisses. I believe each of us has them in our lives. But perhaps the dirt pile is so large we have either forgotten the kisses, or we simply cannot see them. Some have given up hope that they will ever be kissed. However, as long as we are still breathing, the divine kiss will come if we will but ask.

But this makes sense to me: If my imperfect mother could do such an extraordinary thing, kissing my daddy again, and forgiving him and loving him again, well then there must be more out there. And whatever it is that was within her, is within all of us.

If a total reprobate like Victor is loved by this God, in spite of all of Victor's dirt, then perhaps there is hope for the rest of us reprobates.

The source of this love must go back to the first cause. This uncaused cause has to be more than matter, molecules, and gases. Somehow it must have love within it. This eternal being must have the capacity to kiss.

The problem for me now is not whether God exists. People are much too complex for all of this to be an accident, a result of a really big bang. C.S. Lewis once surmised in *God in the Dock* that if we are all an accident, then the thinking that we are all an accident is an accident, and who could trust that to make any sense?

> If the solar system was brought about by an accidental collision, then the appearance of organic life on this planet was an accident too. If so, all our present thoughts are mere accidents... And this holds true for the thoughts of the materialists and astronomers as well for anyone else's. But if their thoughts–i.e. of Materialism and Astronomy–are merely accidental by-products, why should we believe them to be true?[6]

See why I love to read C.S. Lewis?

No, my question for God is not "Do you exist?" The question for me now is, "Where are you when the innocents are being slaughtered?" And the God of the dirt has answers, and they might surprise us a bit.

For now, as we begin this journey into the presence of God, one thought helps me continue the quest and have a peace that is real: *Without dirt, it would be really difficult to slide into home.*

Did God Make a Mistake? Or the God of Regret

Think, O man, think; rejoice and exalt, the first high cause.

—Tommaso Campanella

The verse that stuns me and then stumps me is Genesis 6:6 (NIV), which says, "The Lord regretted that he had made human beings on the earth, and his heart was deeply troubled."

All attempts to describe God fall short. Think about it. If you were infinite God, how would you communicate to finite humans your character and your personality? It isn't like this, but it is... How do we as parents communicate to our little children the truths we see so clearly about life, but that they do not and cannot possibly 'get' yet? I once tried to explain to our then three-year-old daughter, Sara, the logic behind my yelling at a television set when my team was losing yet another game.

"Daddy, why are you yelling? Can the Astros hear you?" Little did she know that my yelling actually helped my team. One day she might understand, but I doubt it. Her mother never has understood it.

There are times we humans cannot understand some things, as long as we are limited by this body of ours. But the mind God gave me at least attempts to grasp some of who God is.

I doubt if Genesis 6:6 will be totally understood by anyone from Augustine to Anselm to C.S. Lewis to Donald Miller or Rob Bell or even Billy Graham. I do not profess to have special insight into its meaning either. So if you happen to disagree, so be it. If no one disagrees, all of us would be in trouble.

MEMO

To: Holy God

From: David

Date: Often

Subject: More Questions

With all respect to you, Holy God, I have a few observations and questions concerning the verse in Genesis. I know that your existence does not depend on my understanding. You are the uncaused first cause—the totally self-existent One. You are not dependent on anything else for your existence. Whether I or anyone else 'gets' you has absolutely nothing to do with whether or not you exist. I do not 'get' women, but we all know that women do indeed exist.

I believe that you must exist. No other explanation of how we got here is possible. Something cannot come from nothing. Something had to have always been here. That something thus must be infinite, self-existent, and the source of all that exists. That something is you. It is your basic definition.

You decided to create us. Certainly you had good reasons. For years I have assumed you are all-knowing. You have told us that you are everywhere and that you know everything. I read it in Psalm 139.

I am assuming that when you created humans on this earth that you somehow knew of things to come. You certainly knew that we, given free choice, would someday blow it. We would choose sin and choose it often.

When you said you regretted that you created us and that your heart was filled with pain, why were you surprised? Could it be that the depth of the rebellion shocked you? Were you hoping that your instincts were wrong, that perhaps humans would say no to the evil one you let tempt them?

Or perhaps you knew, but your love forced you into creating us? Could it be that until the rebellion actually happened, even you could not totally feel it? Even though this goes against my previously held concepts of you, I like this explanation.

When my wife and I were expecting our first child, we knew his life would not be perfect. A day would come when he would look us in the eye and say something like, "No!" So although we knew that day would come, we were incapable of feeling the depth of his rebellion until it actually happened.

We also knew the day(s) would come when he would be hurt. Others would hurt him, and life would be unfair. A disease, a natural disaster, others' selfishness, his own bad choices, something, at some time, in some way would hurt him deeply. And these hurts would not be a one-time happening.

All parents know those days will come. But how could we ever feel the depth of the pain until it happens?

So is that what happened to you God? You brought children into this world out of your heart of love. You knew the risks involved and the pain to come. But you could not feel this pain until...? Thanks for listening—you always do. –David

Years ago, we discovered one of our children had been hurt by a friend of the family. We, his mother and I, experienced the expected emotions. Our hearts were filled with anger at the one who hurt him. And indeed, our hearts were filled with an indescribable, deep pain.

Our child was deeply wounded. His mind was filled with confusion and uncertainties. The results are too much to describe here.

Our pain, as his parents, was heightened in one undeniable fact: We, his mother and father, brought him into this world. We were and are responsible. All his pain and hurt and confusion goes back to us. No, we did not sin against him, as did the one who hurt him. And no, we are not to blame for someone else's sinful choices.

As his father, my responsibility was to protect him, especially from evil. But I did not. Perhaps I could not. There are numerous good reasons that make logical sense as to why I did not. In fact, even perfect parents cannot protect their children from all their hurts and the pain. It appears that God, the perfect Father, has a bunch of children who have been hurt. Perhaps we are more like God than we imagine.

This I know: no matter what the reasons are for my children's hurts, I remain their father. I am responsible. It is my fault they are in this world. And because of this, parents will do whatever it takes to help their children and to protect them. We will spend all we possess if necessary. We will, as we like to say, take a bullet for any one of our children. All parents worth anything feel this way.

So back to Genesis 6. Surely God regretted that he had made us, and certainly his heart was filled with pain. For one thing, he knew the blessings that humans were missing in their rebellion. They were missing what they were created for, which was a relationship with him, their Creator, Provider, Father. He also knew what *he* was missing. Dynamic, personal relationships enrich both parties, even if the other party is God. The result of missing this essential blessing of relationship with the Life-giver is, of course, death. God, in case you have forgotten, simply hates death.

But another reason lurks: *he* was responsible. He was the reason they were alive. Without him they would not exist. The text states, "He regretted that He had made human beings." It is as if God was saying he wished he had never done it; that he had made a mistake. At least that is how he was feeling at that time. In a way it makes sense. The source of life and love desires to create those whom he can love and who can love him in return.

All of that results in life. When those who are created for life and love refuse that, the end result of death is the exact opposite, the antithesis of what God intended. Grief and pain residing in the infinite source (God) should be expected. God's wrath also enters there, for his wrath makes sense. Humans, made to participate in the divine nature, reject the opportunity and choose death! Would you be a bit wrathful if that happened to you?

The above words do not exactly correspond to previously held concepts of God. Yet God knows that better than I have explained it. I sure hope he does, for if not then he is indeed confused.

An obvious truth is this: the greater the responsibility felt, the greater the response. A friend of mine accidently ran over his granddaughter. Samantha remained alive, but she was severely handicapped. My friend spent thousands and thousands of dollars searching for some kind—any kind—of cure. None was found. She died a few years after the accident. Obviously, great grief, hurt, and pain followed. Why did Gerald, my friend, do everything in his power to save his granddaughter, more than any other? Two reasons–he loved her, and he felt the greatest responsibility.

God's response proves that he feels a great responsibility. He gave his only Son. I have often wondered why God didn't have more than one son. I think I now understand a little better. His response could not be scripted better. There could be no story as compelling as this one.

As his only Son hung on that cross, Jesus uttered familiar words. Those words make a lot of sense to me now. To me at least, they explain why God is so full of grace–why he never lets go of us, why he never gives up. It explains his relentless pursuit of us, why it is never too late as long as we are breathing. God understands his role in our being here. He grasps the undeniable fact: he brought us into this world, and only he can rectify the problem. We do not grasp the enormity of our sin problem. He does. "Father, forgive them, for they do not know what they are doing" (Luke 23:34, NIV).

More Questions?

My God, my God, why have you forsaken me? Why are you so far from saving me, so far from my cries of anguish?

Psalm 22:1 (NIV)

The last chapter hopefully has sparked many questions. I can think of a few immediately.

1. Is it right for the created being (me) to question boldly the Creator (God)? Is there a line we dare not cross in our questions? Is it safer to just believe and accept and not try to figure anything out? Or are questions part of our makeup and necessary for faith to grow? And do I ask too many questions?

2. Why did you create us? You stated that your heart was grieved that you made us. Didn't you have a choice? If you knew our rebellion would come, then why do it? I am compelled at times to ask the question Job asked long ago: "Why then did you bring me out of the womb? I wish I had died before any eye saw me. If only I had never come into being, or had been carried straight from the womb to the grave" (Job 10:18,19 NIV).

3. Can't you do all things? I thought you are all-powerful. If you are, why not fix it so we would not rebel? Why not create us to always make the right choices?

4. Do you feel any guilt at all for having created us? Not guilt in the sense of guilt for sin. Though there is much I do not understand about you, I believe I know at least this much, that you are holy, and that you cannot sin. Perhaps the word should be *responsibility.* Could this be the reason you appear to be relentless in your pursuit of us? And could this have anything to do with your immense love, mercy, grace, and patience? Is this connected in any way with your giving me chance after chance, why your forgiveness seems to know no bounds?

Certainly there are more questions we could ask. But these should suffice for now. To many people, the very asking of these questions borders on blasphemy. I understand their thinking. There is an accusatory tone to many of these questions. How dare the created being talk to the Creator in such a manner!

One example from Jesus might help here. His anguished cry from the cross is the apex of *why* questions directed to God. With each word, the knife sinks deeper into the heart of the Father.

"My God, my God, Why have you forsaken me?" (Matthew 27:46 NIV). Twice he reminded his Father that the Father was *his* God. The tone of the question is indeed accusatory: the Father had forsaken the only Son; the Father could have chosen *not* to forsake his Son. The Father, according to the question, quite possibly made a mistake.

The question remains, is the asking of tough, honest questions from the creature to the Creator permissible, and if it is, could it be beneficial and perhaps necessary for our faith?

Jesus shows us that being brutally honest with our feelings to Holy God is indeed permitted. Some could argue that Jesus was not a created being, thus the analogy falls short. But Jesus was fully man on this earth, and we are to follow in his footsteps. He is presented as the person we were meant to emulate. And in addition, there are many other biblical characters that give us permission to ask the tough questions to God. The evidence is overwhelming. God can take our honest outbursts of angst, confusion, and anger, and even our accusations.

I not only believe the asking of these questions is permitted and beneficial, I am at least leaning toward the theory that being brutally honest with God might just be necessary for a growing, vital faith, a faith that can truly change our lives and others' lives, as well.

Thank God for Conflict

> After a heated argument on some trivial matter Nancy [Astor] shouted, "If I were your wife I would put poison in your coffee!" Whereupon Winston [Churchill] answered, "And if I were your husband I would drink it."
>
> —John Fellows Akers

Seeking a relationship with any human being is an adventure. For many years, my wife and I have been privileged to be involved in working with marriages in crisis, through many different venues. In one class we lead, most couples come saying that this is their last chance to salvage their marriage. Of course, we feel no pressure!

The results have been staggering, in spite of the imperfections of its leaders. We see hopeless marriages turn around and experience a fresh start and have learned that for intimacy to develop in any relationship, conflict must become an ally, not an enemy. The reason should be obvious–conflict in any relationship that endures and that enriches is inevitable. Why? Because the parties involved are human, and they are different. Conflict in relationships is not the problem. No, problems arise when couples *avoid* the conflict, or handle the conflict in inappropriate ways.

Willard J. Harley Jr., in *Fall in Love Stay in Love,* discusses in detail what he calls the "3 states of mind in marriage" – Intimacy, Conflict, and Withdrawal (see pages 151-162). Most marriages have some kind of Intimacy at some point in their relationship. After a period of time, Conflict enters the picture. If the Conflict is ignored or not dealt with in a healthy manner, Withdrawal will slowly creep in. Most couples we see are without question at the very end of the Withdrawal stage. How do we help lead them back to Intimacy?

Well, as much as it hurts, they simply must go back through Conflict. They cannot go around the Conflict stage to get back to Intimacy. That would short-circuit the healing of their marriage. Again, the journey from Withdrawal to Intimacy must travel back through the Conflict, but this time by handling the Conflict in such a way that Intimacy can be stronger than ever.

Squarely facing problems in marriage is not an easy, pleasant experience at the time. However, the results can be life changing, and marriage saving. But the process necessitates pain. The pain comes in part from total honesty, full revelations, nothing held back. To have a dynamic marriage, I simply must be honest with my feelings with Debbie. There must be a safe place for me to share anything with her. I need to feel that no matter what I am struggling with, I have her permission to share. Of course, I need to do it with sensitivity and consideration.

I will never forget the couple who had announced to friends and family alike their upcoming divorce. A few of their friends, without their knowing it, made arrangements for them to come see us, with deep consequences if they did not at least attempt to save the marriage. So they reluctantly came, with no intention of doing anything to save their marriage.

Nothing apparently changed during our time together. As they were flying back home, the husband broke the silence. "Look, I know this is too late and that our marriage is over, but I need to tell you something. You deserve the truth. I had an affair a couple of years ago. It has been over for a year. I deeply regret it and am so sorry. I never meant to hurt you."

She sat in silence for a minute and then finally spoke. Her words shocked him. "I don't blame you for having an affair. I have been a terrible wife. I am so sorry for all these years that I have made life miserable for you. I hope you can forgive me."

More, of course, was said. This couple decided to work on their marriage. They forgave each other, went to counseling, and eight years later, as I write these words, they are still together, still working on their marriage. They say they have never been happier.

They had to go through the conflict and not around it. Being truthful with each other and with themselves involved much pain, but it was indeed worth it.

God created the marriage relationship. He desires husband and wife to be *one*. This is true intimacy. I am convinced that one of the reasons God created marriage was to give us a taste for what heaven will be. He knows life is tough. So he creates marriage, including the ultimate intimate action–the sexual relationship–as a respite in the midst of life. Could it be that the closest we are to heaven on this earth is when husband and wife enjoy the ultimate intimate action?

"If that is so," one person told me when she heard this theory, "then perhaps I do not want to go to heaven." However, to be clear, I am not claiming that there will be sex in heaven, but there will be lots of intimacy. "For now we see only a reflection as in a mirror; then we shall see face to face. Now I know in part; then I shall know fully, even as I am fully known" (1 Corinthians 13:12, NIV).

The woman who wanted no part of a heaven with sex in it was being serious. But if her sex life had been as it was intended, with real intimacy and closeness, then her opinion might indeed change. We humans have messed up the ideal. But to many who have experienced marriage for what it was intended, not perfect but indeed intimate, this connection makes sense.

The marriage relationship mirrors and imitates God's relationship with us (see the book of Hosea and Ephesians 5 for examples). The model of "Intimacy, Conflict, and Withdrawal" perfectly parallels God and us. Humans are created for intimate relationships with their Creator.

Conflict enters when humans are human and God is God. For one thing, we are different: Wise vs. foolish; all-knowing vs. partly knowing; holy vs. sinful. We do not understand his silence, or his responses. We live in a fallen world, which is all we really know. He was there when the world had not yet fallen, when it was the way it was supposed to be. He sees with infinite eyes through all eternity; we only see now, today. Conflict is piled upon more conflict.

Then there is the old sin issue. We freely choose to sin, and sin breaks his heart far more than we can imagine. The gulf widens between us. He yearns to be near us, to walk in the garden with us again, yet our sin keeps blocking the intimacy from developing.

Couples come in to counseling crying, "But we are so different!" Books discussing these differences make millionaires of their authors. If men and women are so different, as different as Mars is from Venus, then what about God and humans? God is from forever, humans are from a beginning.

Conflict? Of course there is conflict. Withdrawal from God naturally ensues.

The pathway back to the Creator must then involve going through conflict. And that means honesty with all my sins, all my confusion, and yes, all my questions for God. And really, once we see and admit our common deficiencies in this thing called "living," men and women may see that there are three letters the same in our descriptive nouns, and only two letters that are different, and that they spell *wo*! Once we see our common failures, we might just work out those necessary differences, which we label "conflict."

How ridiculous to have these questions deep in our very souls, and feel as if the all-knowing God would somehow be upset with us for asking. He already knows! He is God!

The Wrestler, the Complainer, and an Excuse Maker

> Then the man said, "Your name will no longer be Jacob, but Israel, because you have struggled with God and with humans and have overcome."
>
> Genesis 32:28 (NIV)

Scripture is filled with honest dialogue and even battles between the Creator and the created. Reading these passages amazes me at times, scares me at other times. God does not seem to hold back how he feels, does he? God does not withdraw. And those who are recorded in scripture rarely hold back either. In fact, it appears that when the conflict between God and humans is addressed head on, with open and honest hearts, great faith, love, and devotion of the creature to the Creator multiplies.

THE WRESTLER

A man named Jacob once had an all-night wrestling match with a man, and did not lose (Genesis 32). Jacob claimed the man was God, for he had seen God face to face and lived (32:30). Weary from the battle, the God figure appeared to cheat. He wrenched Jacob's hip to gain an advantage, yet Jacob would not quit. Finally, God gave up the fight, saying basically "Enough!"

Nice story, isn't it? Does it fit with traditional views of God? Not mine.

God cannot win a wrestling match? God cheats to gain an advantage? God basically gives up, satisfied with a tie?

Ah, but the story is not about a cheating, weak, give-up-when-the-going-gets-tough God. God is none of the above. The God who created something—a lot of somethings—out of nothing, could certainly have whipped Jacob. I am not really sure about God resorting to unfair tactics, except to test the tenacity and the determination of Jacob. And I know that God is not a quitter. Just one look at me proves God never gives up on hopeless people. He is certainly no quitter.

No, the story is about a man who feels guilt and shame brought about by selfish, sinful choices of his past. Anyone relate? It centers on one who is filled with fear, for in his mind he is about to meet head-on the consequences of his past (Esau from whom he had stolen his blessing). It is about a desperate man doing a desperate thing. I will fight with God for his blessing—for the blessing I have is ill-gotten gain, he seems to say. And I will not stop, even when the pain is excruciating in my hip, until he blesses me.

So God blessed Jacob, and changed his name to Israel, the meaning of which staggers me. *Israel* means "he struggles with God."

"Then the man said, 'Your name will no longer be Jacob, but Israel because you have struggled with God and with men and have overcome'" (Genesis 32:28). God apparently appreciates a good fight entered into with noble purposes.

THE COMPLAINER

Listen to a man whose name I can never pronounce correctly. His name is Habakkuk. He is one of the few in history whose name appears in Holy scripture. He knew God, and had a great faith in God. The end of his short book is one of the great faith passages ever:

> I heard and my heart pounded, my lips quivered at the sound; decay crept into my bones, and my legs trembled. Yet I will wait patiently for the day of calamity to come on the nation invading us. Though the fig tree does not bud and there are no grapes on the vines, though the olive crop fails and the fields produce no food, though there are no sheep in the pen and no cattle in the stalls, yet I will rejoice in the Lord, I will be joyful in God my Savior. The Sovereign Lord is my strength; he makes my feet like the feet of a deer, he enables me to go on the heights.
>
> Habakkuk 3:16–19 (NIV)

That sounds like a man experiencing a walk with God that works. It is indeed intimate. Going to the heights with God? Knowing God is with us in every situation, no matter how dark it might be? That's what I desire. Shouldn't it be like that? If God is real, if you and I were created to have a dynamic relationship with Holy God, should we not all go to the heights with God? It is what we were created to be, to do, to live!

So how did Habakkuk get there? What was his secret? There are undoubtedly many reasons Habakkuk had such a relationship with God that resulted in unwavering trust in the midst of such loss. *Intimacy* might be too mild a word to describe their relationship.

But a casual reading of the first chapter reveals the deep conflict Habakkuk felt toward his God. He withheld nothing from God; his words are filled with accusations, questions, confusion, and feelings of betrayal. During that time of questioning, I doubt if

Habakkuk would have willingly sat around a campfire singing "How Great is Our God." But perhaps he would have, for his relationship with God permitted the tough questions. Conflicted feelings were part of that dynamic, intimate relationship. Listen to the honesty of his soul as he seeks answers for the despair he feels.

> How long, O LORD, must I call for help, but you do not listen? Or cry out to you, "Violence!" but you do not save? Why do you make me look at injustice? Why do you tolerate wrong? Destruction and violence are before me; there is strife, and conflict abounds. Therefore the law is paralyzed, and justice never prevails. The wicked hem in the righteous, so that justice is perverted.
>
> Habakkuk 1:2–4 (NIV)

Habakkuk's words remind me of numerous conversations I have had with God. To Habakkuk his relationship with God deserved such honesty. It is a compliment to my wife when I bare my soul to her. I am telling her I love her too much to accept anything less than a dynamic, intimate relationship. The same can be said with friends, co-workers, or bosses. This honesty is also declaring a deep trust that my God can take it, that in fact he desires it.

The conflict Habakkuk felt was not easily resolved. It was no five-minute conversation. God answered his first complaint with what should be reassuring words from the Almighty.

> Look at the nations and watch–and be utterly amazed. For I am going to do something in your days that you would not believe, even if you were told. I am rising up the Babylonians, that ruthless and impetuous people, who sweep across the whole earth to seize dwelling places not their own.
>
> Habakkuk 1:5–6 (NIV)

If I may paraphrase God's response to his friend, "I hear you Habakkuk. You seem upset. I am going to take care of all your concerns. You will be totally amazed by how I handle the problem, using evil Babylon to solve the problem. Thanks for sharing your concerns with me."

One would think that response would appease the concerns of Habakkuk. Holy God had heard Habakkuk's complaint. He had responded. How many of our prayers appear unheard by God? How often have I poured out my soul to God and waited... and waited... and heard nothing? I would be thrilled at the response he gave Habakkuk—at least God would have spoken to me!

But Habakkuk was one stubborn human. God's response was not good enough for him. In fact, it almost makes matters worse. The audacity of Habakkuk in light of the Holy God's response is shocking, yet it should inspire us. Habakkuk didn't understand God's answer. It was not good enough for him. Perhaps it should have been, but it simply wasn't. So he continued his relentless questioning of the Creator. Why? Because nothing short of total honesty was a necessity in his relationship with God. Somehow Habakkuk understood that. His faith was cemented in his knowledge that God was okay with it.

> Lord, are you not from everlasting? My God, my Holy One, you will never die. You, Lord, have appointed them to execute judgment; you, my Rock, have ordained them to punish. Your eyes are too pure to look on evil; you cannot tolerate wrongdoing. Why then do you tolerate the treacherous? Why are you silent while the wicked swallow up those more righteous than themselves?
>
> Habakkuk 1:12-13 (NIV)

To Habakkuk, God's actions were not consistent with God's character. Note the accusations: "Why do you, the infinite and Holy God, tolerate the treacherous? Why are you silent while the wicked swallow up those more righteous than themselves?" I am trying to understand you, God. But it still makes no sense to me.

Have you ever dared talk to God like that? I know you have felt those emotions. But to act upon them with real words and cries to the everlasting God? Why does that type of conversation scare us? If it does, I submit the reason could be that you have never tried it.

I have tried it, because I cannot pretend any longer. I was tired of playing the game with God, disguising it as great faith. I falsely defined *great faith* as "never questioning God." That is not the biblical definition of faith. If it is, then Moses, and Habakkuk, and a host of other spiritual Hall of Famers, and even Jesus failed the faith test.

So there was God trying his best to listen to a complaint from one he loved. He responded; he was not silent. He promised to take care of the problem that Habakkuk presented. But Habakkuk did not like the plan that the all-wise, all-knowing God devised. So a mere human, with limited understanding and by all accounts woefully short of his God's wisdom and experience, complained again. What might you have done if you had been God?

God's response is found in chapter two. "Take some notes," God says. "Make it plain so others can spread the news. There is an answer that will deal with all your complaints. Trust me; wait for it."

God's patience in the midst of a complaining prophet was extraordinary. The result: Habakkuk's praise and devotion, and finally unwavering faith (chapter 3).

Conflict evolved into deep intimacy.

THE EXCUSE MAKER

It is believed that A.W. Tozer literally wrote *The Pursuit of God* while on his knees, and he did not have a laptop. Note these words in the introduction (not written by Tozer):

> Perhaps the continued usefulness of this book can be attributed to the writer's great spiritual discovery that to seek God does not narrow one's life, but brings it, rather, to the level of highest possible fulfillment[7].

Though Tozer does not specifically mention questioning God in this pursuit, the principle is the same. We are to go "hard after God." To seek God with everything we have would include seeking him with all our doubts, confusion, questions, and emotions. There is a season for everything, even a time to wrestle with the very one who created us (Jacob).

At times we may think this *hard seeking* after God is not worth it. It hurts! It should not be this difficult. God could and should just show up and reassure me, we might think. But this God-and-I thing rarely comes easy. Why? It's because real relationships between real people have real issues and differences. Intimacy develops in the foxhole when two people face difficulties together and struggle together. We know this to be true in human relationships. Thus, it must be true in God-Human relationships as well. This seeking is not restricted to seeking to know whether or not God exists. It would certainly include that. But, as Tozer says, "We have been snared in the coils of a spurious logic that insists that if we have found Him, we need no more seek Him."[8] Once we find God, the opposite is true. The seeking should intensify. In marriage, the same principle applies.

I stated earlier that God's existence is not a problem for me at this time. It used to be, but no longer. For many people the question of his existence has not been resolved. If that is the case, seek him. Ask the tough questions. If he does not exist, then he won't strike you down for the questions, for he does not exist. If he indeed exists, then he will honor your honest seeking. The open heart that seeks God can and will find him. One cannot really lose by seeking hard after God.

Habakkuk, Jacob, and others who boldly questioned God were still seeking. They knew he existed. They did not grasp everything about him, nor did they agree with everything he did. To come to an agreement with anyone with whom we disagree requires communication, seeking to understand. Even with humans, total understanding is not a prerequisite for love and acceptance. However, the closer we are drawn into the heart and soul of another, the more we understand, and if we feel that we have been heard, then often that is enough, even in the midst of not quite "getting" her or him.

How much more is it so with infinite, holy God? I repeat, I need a few "Aha!" mountaintop moments with God. I need to understand some things about him. And though I will never totally get there, the seeking is indeed part of getting there.

Moses is a great illustration. I challenge you to read Exodus 32 and 33, attempting to have a clean slate concerning your concept of God. If all we know of God is derived from these two chapters, what will our concept be of God?

Moses knew God existed. After all, "The Lord would speak to Moses face to face as one speaks with his friend" (Exodus 33:11). That is the same Moses who tried every excuse he could discover to turn down God's job for him (Exodus 3, 4). He indeed is a master excuse maker.

The context of Exodus 32 and 33 is the sin of the people when Moses was on the mountain, receiving the law from God. We read of the intense hurt and, thus, anger of God at his people. We heard how God had had it, that he would destroy the people because of their rebellion. We saw Moses boldly dialoguing with God, pleading with him to reconsider. Moses engaged in daring rhetoric: "But now, please forgive their sin—but if not, then blot me out of the book you have written" (Exodus 32:32).

We are shocked to discover that God was undecided about what he was going to do (Exodus 33:5). He told Moses to take the people and go to the Promised Land, but he was not going to go with them (Exodus 33:1ff). Why? It was because if God went with them, he might destroy them. In other words, God could not trust his own emotions!

Moses knew that he must have God's presence with him, or he would fail in his mission. Thus he pled with God, culminating with the desire of his heart, sounding as if he was demanding this from God: "Now show me your Glory!" (v. 18).

I am not claiming to be Moses; but I am claiming to be a human, created by God as Moses was. There is something within us, dare we say, that demands to see God, that desires to know him intimately, and that is determined to realize more and more his presence. So we can say with Moses, "Lord, show us your glory!"

Tozer says what we need to see is that God is a personality. We, being created in his image, are also personalities. As persons we are the only part of God's creation that can even think in terms of disagreeing with God, of questioning him. Dogs and cats never even think of saying no to God; neither do they have the privilege or opportunity to say yes to the Creator. We humans are privileged and honored to search, to go after God with all of our personality. Going hard after God can at times be painful, but is indeed worth it.

In his introduction, Tozer discussed the uselessness of the Bible if we miss the source of the power. It is not in mere words, he said, but God himself who feeds our souls. We dare not miss the intent of God—intimacy between the Holy God and us, his sinful creation.

> For it is not mere words that nourish the soul, but God himself, and unless and until the hearers find God in personal experience they are not the better for having heard the truth. The Bible is not an end in itself, but a means to bring men to an intimate and satisfying knowledge of God, that they may enter into Him, that they may delight in His Presence, may taste and know the inner sweetness of the very God himself in the core and center of their hearts[9].

Go Ahead, Turn Your Head—You Can Do It

If you can dream it, you can do it.

—Walt Disney

The number one person I should have a dynamic relationship with has to be the Creator. I love the quote from A.W. Tozer noted in the previous chapter, "That they may enter into Him, that they may delight in His Presence, may taste and know the inner sweetness of the very God himself in the core and center of their hearts."[10] Is this not what we long for? Certainly the God of the universe did not call us to simply attend a worship service once a week and go through some form of worship ritual. His call for us is a call to life, to the real meaning of life. Certainly, the Sunday experience of worship could help us to that end. But the Sunday experience is not the desired outcome—the outcome deeply desired by the Creator is that we realize the true meaning of our existence.

That makes sense to me. But why is it so difficult? Why must pain and conflict play such big roles?

In the last chapter we talked about the connection and thus the similarities between the God relationship and the marriage relationship. There are certainly tough times in both. But there has to be those simple times when it works, almost without thinking. I grow weary of intense thinking all the time. I do not think our brains were made to only focus on trigonometry and calculus; I need some good ole P.E. classes when the coach throws out the ball and says, "Just have fun boys" (I think that might have happened once while I was in school, maybe, but probably not).

How do I, a very ordinary human, experience those moments with him that I know he is here, and I am here with him? It cannot be just in the thinking mode.

Let's see, I pray to him very respectfully. I sing to him, real praise songs. I go to one of his churches, if I can find the right one among so many choices. I try not to miss many church services, unless it's Super Bowl Sunday or something else important. I try not to say, "O my God" as every single person on TV does forty times in thirty minutes. Things like that.

And yet, we know a *but* is coming. That experience does not exactly feel right, if that's all it is. At some point, in some way, the relationship with God must result in real experiences.

As I write these words, Debbie and I are flying to Washington, DC. She has been my bride for thirty-six years. Like most marriages, we have had our good times and bad times.

I spend much of my time counseling those about to be married, those married and struggling with each other, and those married and hanging on by a thread, or worse. One day I was talking to a couple trying to save their marriage. It was one of those *worst* sessions.

"What motivated you to come see me?" I foolishly asked.

"Well," he began, "when we started shooting at each other, we decided it was time."

"Oh really," I suspiciously asked. "With real guns?"

"Of course," she responded incredulously. "What else would one shoot with? When I shot at my husband, after he shot at me first, he ducked behind a table, and the bullet missed him and struck our mantle, shattering it. It was then we both realized we needed help. So we stopped the shooting."

I didn't but should have said, "Seems to me you should have realized that you needed help when you first purchased those 'his' and 'her' guns, and when you wore them around your waist as Matt Dillon did, always ready to shoot back if your spouse started it." Anyway, the point of all this is that we have to simplify things every now and then. If I only deal with gun-totin' couples all the time, I just might give up trying to help anyone, or spend a lot of money on those metal detector devices.

So back to the plane ride.

Seated next to me across the aisle to my right were three young women—"young" being younger than we by about twenty-five years. They appeared to be fairly good looking. Okay, they were *really* good-looking. After a few minutes, they got up from their seats, standing with, shall we say, their backsides dangerously close to me. I thought for a second to sneak a peak, then stopped, and decided to look the other way, to my left. My bride was asleep at that moment and would never have known if I had looked. And after all, as many have said, there is nothing wrong with looking if you do not touch.

Deep in my heart, I know that kind of thinking is false. So I decided to honor my precious wife. I looked at her instead. (I do not want anyone to think I have always done the right thing in these situations. I see no good that can come from outright lying at this point in my life or in this book.) When I gazed at my sleeping wife, I saw an incredible wonder. I saw the one whom has always stood by me, always believed in me. I gazed upon the mother of our four children, who has sacrificed it seems daily for them. I stared at one who has been there with me through triumphs and defeats, pain and despair, heartbreak and heartaches. She was there when those I trusted betrayed me. She held me when Dad died, and recently when Mom joined our Father in heaven. She took care of my mom, Nana, when she was so sick. She comforted me when Josiah died, and she was a rock for me. Together, on a daily basis, we marvel at the absolute wonder and beauty of our four precious granddaughters. I can share those moments with none other. She has loved me when I was so disrespectful to her, when I spoke harsh words, was inconsiderate and selfish. And to top it all off, she is one of the few who laughs at my attempts at humor when I teach. And that is no small feat.

She just keeps on loving me. I really don't get it, her loyalty and love for me. I do not deserve it.

When I turned to my left and looked at her, I saw a fifty-five-year-old grandmother—a fantastic "Nonni," who has put on a few extra pounds over the years and who gets her graying hair touched up every month, whose to-do lists drive me crazy at times. I saw the one with whom I have fought with more than any other human on earth, and the one to whom I have apologized more often than all others.

When I decided to turn away from the younger women to my right to look at this Nonni to my left, I honored her, and in so doing I honored my God, who many years ago gave her to me as a gift. "Here is the wife you asked for, David," he said to me that day in 1972 when I asked her to leave her parents and live the adventure of life with me. "You love her and her alone, you hear me? You honor her."

And by the way, when I scanned her face, her beauty simply blew away those younger women to my right. With no offense intended toward those young ladies, you just do not measure up. My bride is the most beautiful woman on earth.

She is all I need and desire. I have the best, and I intend to honor her more and more.

So today I have understood more about this tantalizing, incredibly difficult relationship with God. It does not always have to be complicated. It was quite simple really—the slight turning of my head, then the thoughtful reflection of this treasure, and the realization of the One who gave her to me.

The Look of Life

It's not what you look at that matters, it's what you see.

—Henry David Thoreau

It was a few minutes before midnight when the *look* returned, quite unexpectedly I might add. I recall vividly all the other instances of the look on that face and the pure joy that engulfed it. Each of them centered upon the general theme of family. There were the days in the doctors' offices when we discovered we were pregnant. There was her confident smile when she held her babies for the first time, when she brought them home and walked through the door of our house, carrying that incredible bundle of joy, fear, expectation, hope, and dreams, and of course the birth of all our grandbabies.

The look would make a surprise visit at times, like when I stumbled upon the exact words I needed to say, at just the right moment, and with just the right tone. I believe she has experienced that three times in our thirty-eight years together. Or when a son would leap up from the table after dinner and exclaim, "No, Mom, let me. You work much too hard; I will clean up the kitchen tonight." That fateful event remains singular, February 10, 1991, a day after he forgot his mother's birthday.

It is difficult, if not impossible, to adequately describe that look. It is similar to losing something valuable, searching frantically for it, almost giving up hope, and then when all seems lost, to stumble upon it right in front of you, perhaps when you were not looking any longer. All seems right in your world for that moment.

Your teams win the World Series and the Super Bowl in the same year; your children share their toys, respect one another, and go to bed thirty minutes early and sleep till noon on Saturday; your boss promotes you and praises you in front of everyone; Arnold Palmer calls and wants to play a round of golf with you at Augusta; they discover ice cream and chocolate have no calories and reduce the risk of a heart attack.

In a slightly deeper vein, the look on your face seems to shout "Aha! So this is what it means to live; this now is the meaning of life; this must be what God is really all about. I see it, really; it is so clear."

Perhaps the look conveys "the peace that passes all understanding"; the love unimaginable; the hope that is rekindled, forgiveness undeserved.

Just this week a husband shared the wonder of that look at a most unexpected moment. Three months ago he discovered his wife of thirty-one years had been having an affair. After much grief, anguish, anger, remorse, repentance, promises made again, counseling appointments, and more tears, he couldn't take it any longer. Storming out of the bedroom, he went to sleep on the couch. The man who had promised a second chance to his fallen, "I-am-so-very-sorry" wife gave up. He would not, perhaps *could* not, even begin to imagine really forgiving her. The marriage was over.

After an hour of not sleeping at all, he heard footsteps coming from the bedroom. His fallen bride quietly came to the couch, sat down, and gently placed her head on his chest. Nothing was said. After fifteen minutes or so, he began to look at her. He saw her eyes, and something changed. He could not explain it; he had no desire to explain it. He just knew he still loved her. And she felt the same.

In that moment, life somehow makes sense. That is what it means to live—love, pain, hurt, raw emotions, conflict, death, feelings, and finally forgiveness, followed by reconciliation, intimacy, and more forgiveness. Life, and with it, God. Not the god of religions clamoring to be number one, or the god of contradictions, hopelessness, or nonsense. No, this is God, right here in the midst of giving up and confusion.

So back to my *look* moment. There I was, at midnight, straining to stay awake, when the look returned for the surprise visit. Why the look so late on this particular night in 2011?

The back-story explains it clearly. Anyone who knew her story would get it and just might grow a bit from it.

The story began in 1955. Melba and Rich could not have children. Melba ran around with a single woman named Joyce. Joyce could have children. In fact, she had a son with another child on the way. Being unmarried with one child was not particularly smiled upon in the 1950s. Having not learned your lesson and repeating the mistake could really be disastrous. So Joyce, for the love of her two children, gave up the newly born daughter to her friend Melba.

Melba and Rich, though of course far from perfect, were good people and good parents to their adopted daughter, Debbie. Both died in the 1990s. Debbie always felt a nagging emptiness inside. While her adopted parents were alive, she repressed the building desire to find her family, particularly her mother. When I first met Debbie, she was seventeen and a very lonely, only child.

"Would you be my big brother?" she asked me one night, luring me into her net. "I always wanted a big brother and sisters. You know, don't you, that I am adopted and an only child?"

"Sure, I will be your big brother." So, of course, we were married two years later.

Thirty-nine years later, in May of 2011, the story took a dramatic turn. Through incredible hard-to-believe events, somehow we found Debbie's birth mother and arranged to meet her. She was in a nursing home in Pennsylvania, suffering with dementia and a host of other problems. In addition, we were told that Debbie had three sisters, two who were still alive, and an older brother.

The sisters and brother had no idea they had another sibling until the day before. So at midnight, when a cousin sat in our den and shared the news with us about them, that's when I saw the *look* again.

"You mean my two sisters and older brother want to meet me?"

Her face had a different look to it, as if life was somehow more complete now. The hole in her heart was closing. The gnawing emptiness ebbed away. A peace and joy washed over her face in a clearly recognizable form. Awe, joy, wonderment—life the way life was meant to be. People do say I tend to exaggerate everything. That was *not* one of those times. And she had not even met them yet.

In the subsequent days, the look almost took permanent residence as she met her mother and sisters for the first time. It was as if she had known them all her life.

One moment among many speaks for the rest of them. We were driving through the countryside of Pennsylvania, about an hour away from meeting her sisters and mother. The tension, as they say, was indeed mounting when the phone rang. It was Deb's brother calling from Colorado. He could not be there for the meeting and wanted to talk to his newfound sister for the first time.

How did he know what he needed to say? But know he did. "Hello, little sister."

Through her tears she managed those words she had longed to say for fifty-six years: "Hello, big brother." And at that moment, the *look* returned.

The key word about the look, at least to me, is *connection*, which has a lot to do with purpose and meaning in life. We humans were built for connection—connection with fellow-humans, and connection with the One who created us.

As for me, I gladly give up the role of the big brother to Randy, for the look is quite seductive, alluring, and even compelling. For when I see that look, I see God again. I like what I see, and that, I think, is something very good.

A Visit With the Pope(s)

"GETTING" GOD MIGHT BE EASIER THAN WE THINK

> Do not be afraid. Do not be satisfied with mediocrity. Put out into the deep and let down your nets for a catch.
>
> —Pope John Paul II

Not many people are privileged to secure a visit with the Pope. As humbly as I can say this, I hereby declare that I have had a visit with two, that's two, count them, two different Popes. Actually, my whole family was honored to be present with these Popes. They were called John and Jewell Pope, and they lived in the thriving metropolis of Luray, Tennessee. Population: not very many and even less than that. In case you don't know where Luray is, it's about three miles south of Miflin.

Luray has a special place in the hearts of all the students who were blessed to have attended church there. It was a typical small country church building, with a seating capacity of around fifty. Every Sunday during the school year, about one hundred or so students from a nearby university would make the fifteen-minute drive over winding, country back roads to attend church with about six Lurayians. That means it was always a jam-packed building, with many standing throughout the service.

John and Jewell were one of the three local couples who were the permanent members. For years, the Popes would simply love the kids who attended the church. On many Sundays they would have ten to twenty students over for lunch after church. If you went there long enough, your turn would eventually come up, usually about once a semester or so. On special occasions, when attendance was down a little, they would just invite the entire congregation over. On those Sundays, fifty to sixty people would eat at their small, three-bedroom farmhouse.

And the Popes supplied all the food. I truly feel sorry for those who never tasted the food, but especially for those who never experienced the warm, accepting, open hearts of two of God's finest servants. Many of us would frequently visit the Popes during the week as well. We would go over to their house, fish in their pond, eat homemade biscuits, country ham, and red-eye gravy, and do a lot of hugging on Jewell.

I left Tennessee in 1972. Two years later, four hundred miles away in Louisiana, Deb and I were about to be married. We had sent an invitation to the Popes of course, never dreaming they would attend the blessed event. They were well up in years, and they undoubtedly received tons of wedding invitations every summer from the students.

The day of the wedding, the phone rang. It was John Pope. "We're here for the wedding," he began. "How do I get to the church building?"

When they arrived at the building, I greeted them in the lobby.

"You shouldn't have come all this way for my wedding. This is so nice of you. I just can't believe you're here."

"We wouldn't have missed this for anything. We never thought you would get a date, much less convince some girl to marry you."

Thanks a lot, Jewell.

Eleven years passed. We had not seen or heard from the Popes since the wedding. It was then 1985. We had four children, and we took a short trip to visit friends in Tennessee. Coming back, we went through Jackson, and I remembered that the Popes and Luray were not far from there. So we decided to drop in on them.

Luray had not changed a bit. The one store was still standing; the church building was the same. The parking lot still needed paving. But strangers were living in the Popes' house, and the only one home was a teenager, who had no idea what had happened to them.

We pulled into the Luray store parking lot, hoping someone there would know where they lived, and praying that they were still alive. As I entered the store, the owner greeted me. I asked him if John and Jewell Pope still lived in Luray. Nope, he quickly said. "They moved to Lexington a year or so ago. They still come to church here though. Were you one of their students?"

I said yes, feeling proud that outsiders knew all about the Popes' students. I asked for directions to Lexington. He did not know the Popes' address.

Thirty minutes later we arrived in Lexington. I looked up their number and called them from a convenience store. The conversation that follows is almost word for word.

"Is this John Pope?"

"Yep."

"Your wife named Jewell?"

"Yep."

"You got any homemade biscuits and red-eye gravy around?"

"As a matter of fact, I do. We have some leftover from breakfast."

"You got enough to feed my family?"

"How big is your family?"

"Just the wife and four kids."

"Sure, we'll cook some more if we don't have enough."

"Well, where do you live?"

"Where are you?"

"At Johnson's Store on the main highway."

"Can you see the Big Star Store from where you are?"

"Yes, sir. I'm looking at it right now."

"Good. We live just behind it, in a yellow house. You can't miss it."

"Okay. We'll be there in just a minute."

"Looking forward to seeing you. But can you tell me something?"

"What's that, John?"

"Who are you?"

"You'll find out soon enough."

"Okay. We'll be waiting."

Two minutes later as we pulled up in their driveway, there they were, standing on the front porch, arms around each other, waiting. They evidently did not know exactly who was coming; they only knew it had to be one of their former college kids. As we ran up to greet them, tears were already in their eyes. Hugs, tears, more hugs; introducing our children they had never seen. The Lord was with us. None of our kids acted up. They sensed they were in the presence of royalty, for they were.

As we settled into their living room, Jewell told me to look at a huge album on their coffee table. In it were memories and miracles. Letters and pictures from, literally, hundreds of the students that had graced their home and eaten at their table from the past. The messages came from all over the world, from all types of people: teachers, preachers, business owners, housewives, politicians, attorneys, doctors, and missionaries. They all wrote similar messages: "You two have changed our lives. Thank you for teaching us what love is all about; what God is all about. We will never forget you. Happy fiftieth wedding anniversary."

A year before their golden anniversary, the Popes' children had "stolen" their parents' guest books. Every student who had visited their house during their college years were made to sign one of these books and put their hometown by their names. You could not leave unless you signed it. There were hundreds, perhaps thousands of names in those books.

The Popes' children painstakingly searched for every address of the former students. They sent each one a letter, telling them the surprise coming for their parents. Please send a picture of your family and a brief note to Mom and Dad and what they meant to you. "After all," they wrote, "you all were their kids as well."

So Deb and I sat and read the letters, viewed the photos, and remembered the good times. For a moment, dread came over me. I remembered the letter I had received from their kids months earlier, but I knew I had not responded. It seemed that everyone I knew from my college days had a picture and a letter in that book.

As I was about to make my confession and beg for forgiveness, Jewell spoke up. "I think your letter and picture are on the next page, David." She turned the page, and there it was. I looked at my wife, who gave me one of those looks that said, "See why you married me?"

It took over an hour to look through that book. When we finally finished, I asked one of my patented, really dumb questions: "How often do you guys look at this?"

Without hesitation, and in perfect sync, they said, "Every day. Every day."

I think we need a whole lot more Popes in our world.

It's All God's Fault—Really

> The Lord regretted that he had made human beings on the earth, and his heart was deeply troubled.
>
> Genesis 6:6 (NIV)

Let's just get it out in the open: it is God's fault, all of it. There, I've said it, as Job seemed to say a long, long time ago. "If it is not he, then who is it?" (Job 9:24 NIV).

I was born in June of 1950. Though there are numerous things I do not know about my beginnings, this I do know: no one, not my parents and not even God himself, no one asked my permission or my input before I was thrust into this world. I imagine you could say the same thing.

Now this is no little deal. I was born into the home of Tom and Valerie Mathews in a town of about 100,000 people in southeast Texas. Beaumont is about ninety miles from Houston. I did nothing to deserve this location. Tom and Valerie were really good people. Dad spanked me once, and he cried. Mom chased me around the yard numerous times with a switch, but to my recollection never once connected the switch to my bottom.

Looking back, I'm now fairly certain she did not make much of an effort to catch me.

I went to a neighborhood school and played with the other kids who lived on the same street. Mom hung clothes on the line to dry, and we rarely locked our doors. We went to Friday night football games, ate hamburgers and hot dogs on Saturday afternoons, went to church on Sundays, and watched *Leave It to Beaver*, *Father Knows Best*, and *The Andy Griffith Show*, in black and white by the way. Saturdays from April to September were spent watching the *Major League Game of The Week* with Dizzy Dean and Pee Wee Reese announcing. We had three stations to choose from, and only one or two had good reception. The "rabbit ears" antennas were constantly being re-arranged on the TV.

We actually had a "party-line" telephone. That was where you shared the same phone line with someone else. Long before contraptions were invented to listen to others' phone calls, we could, and I did, sneak a listen when the other "party" was talking on the phone. But please do not tell anyone this offense of mine.

When I was thirteen, my favorite college football team in the world won the national championship. When Texas beat Navy and their quarterback Roger Staubach in the Cotton Bowl, I actually thought this:

> I am the luckiest person in the world. If God had given me the opportunity to choose where to be born and to whom, I have would have picked Beaumont, Texas, and Tom and Valerie Mathews. I would pick Roger Koshkin as my best friend, Midford Drive as the place to have a house, and West End Little League as the one and only place to play baseball. I would root for the South Park Greenies, Lamar Tech Cardinals, and Texas Longhorns. I am the envy of everyone in the entire world!

If I had surveyed a million people who were not born in Beaumont, they *all* would indeed desire to change places with me, or so I thought.

I know and you know what happened to change that perception. It is called life. Certain happenings began to change my impressions. Texas lost the next year to Arkansas (by one point) and did not finish number one. South Park lost more than they won, Lamar dropped football, and we moved to Houston. Roger and I became a memory, Mom and Dad hated each other, and Dad moved out. Ann and Richard went to college, pimples invaded my body, and I went to a school of 3,000 kids where I knew no one. To top it all off, I became a Houston Astro and Houston Oiler fan. And if you know anything at all about baseball and football, you now should really feel sorry for me.

I went to my beloved University of Texas (UT), and the Longhorns tied their first game and lost their second. I made two Fs and two Ds in my first semester of college, and even more traumatic, never had one date, for two very good reasons. First, I never asked anyone out on a date; and second, I never said a word to a member of the opposite sex. I had one friend at UT, and because I am now somewhat of a nice person, will not mention his name. But he was, as we said back in the 1960s, one weird dude. Of course, everyone in Austin, Texas, in 1968 was "one weird dude." Okay, everyone in the '60s was weird.

The reason for this inane rambling is that I no longer felt like everyone would trade places with me. However, I would have gladly traded places with just about anyone in the world, except maybe an Aggie or a Sooner. And as all of us over thirty know, the real "fun" was just beginning.

And God questions penetrated my brain.

The one thought that will not leave me, that I cannot explain away, is this: this whole mess of a world is... his fault. Sin is our fault; I know that. God will not and should not take any blame for our choices. *But it is his fault that we* have *those choices.*

I know writing such things makes those around me a bit squeamish. Entertaining such thoughts and actually expressing them cause many around me to duck, look up, leave, and/or not name their kids after me. But to all you God people out there, if it is not the Creator's fault, whose fault is it?

In my profession of preaching and counseling, I have seen those born into outrageously abusive situations. Fathers, stepfathers, uncles, cousins, moms, aunts, and others physically, sexually, and emotionally abusing little ones. Some others are born into extreme poverty or wealth, hatred, love, religion, atheism, skepticism, faith, safety, danger, and on it goes.

In a recent support group I was leading, a woman stood before the group and shared how, when she was ten, her mother held a gun to her (the daughter's) head and pulled the trigger three times, the gun misfired each time, giving the daughter time to run out the door, never to return again. In the same hour, another woman shared how her father had sexually abused her repeatedly, and her mother never believed her. Within minutes of this revelation, another woman shared how her mother repeatedly told her while she was growing up how worthless she was, and how she, the mother, wished her daughter was dead. None of these victims did anything to deserve such inhumane treatment. The only common thread was that they were born into a bad environment.

A few years ago I traveled to Tanzania, and I saw countless villages. One day we visited a typical household. There, in the middle of nowhere, so it seemed, were three huts—one for cooking, one where the kids lived, and then the master bedroom, where the head of the family and his wife lived. There were at least ten to twelve children, all shoeless and wearing Nike T-shirts. After a rousing welcome by the children, the mother invited us in to see her husband, who was dying of cancer, lying in the only room of the master hut. His cancer had gone untreated obviously.

The stench as we entered overcame a few of us. He was full of graciousness and hospitality as he invited all ten of us to sit on his so-called bed, the only furniture in the room. The cancer had eaten a gaping hole in his abdomen, and the description of what we saw must stop there.

Later, our group engaged in a lively discussion about the fairness of all we saw. Who among us would have been any different from those we met if we had been born into that same situation? Who among us *deserved* to be born where we were born and when? The inevitable conclusions to such questions confuse me. Not one of all the people in this world was ever asked their opinion of where they were to be born, or if they *wanted* to be born. No consultation; no negotiation. In my confused moments of trying to figure some of that out, I have imagined a typical entry-into-the-world scenario going something like this, (knowing now that this is *not* the way it went down):

> You are going to be born, and thrust into the world. I know you will not have a daddy around, and your mother is a prostitute. I am sorry to inform you of this, but I know that men will abuse you, and your mom will leave you. You will be raised on the streets and have to scrounge for your daily provision. But now you'd better be good and go to church, and it better be the *right* church. And if you are not good enough, for long enough, then you will spend eternity in a burning hell forever. Now get going; they are waiting for you to enter the world. By the way, have a nice life.

Perhaps that is one of the reasons I have struggled "getting" God. Many in this world have a concept of God similar to that described above. Is there any doubt, if that is their concept, why so many believe that the idea of God is absurd to them? I will say this: if that is the God I am to believe in, then forget it. I refuse to serve and love and give my life to that god (little 'g' intended).

Is the above description even remotely connected to the holy, loving God? I used to think so. But no longer. Although I realize that I can never totally understand the real God, I can and do indeed know that the above description is not accurate.

So are you ready to disown me yet? I hope you don't. But I will again say it: it *really does* all go back to God. If we know that, because there is no other explanation, I believe God understands his role even better. "The Lord regretted that he had made human beings on the earth, and his heart was deeply troubled" (Genesis 6:6 NIV).

The Mustness of Our Existence

> No one has ever seen God; but if we love one another, God lives in us and his love is made complete in us.
>
> 1 John 4:12 (NIV)

The question posed to my college class appeared easy: "If you were hired to build a playground in a park in a neighborhood, and you discovered somehow that a child was going to die in that playground, and he would not die if you did not build it, would you proceed to build it even if they offered you a huge amount of money?"

The only answer of course is "No." Why would I, albeit an imperfect human, even consider building something in which an innocent child would die? If I proceeded to build it in spite of the consequences, what conclusions might one have? The obvious one would be that I am an incredibly selfish person, loving the money I would make on the playground more than a human life.

Let's assume that I am not a selfish person, at least not that selfish. What other reasons might I proceed with the building plans? If I really knew a child was going to die, and I was not a self-absorbed person, then there are no other possible reasons why I would build it.

As the class proceeded to discuss this hypothetical case, most of us sensed what was coming. The class was entitled "Atheism, Agnosticism, and Christianity." We were exploring all the best arguments against the existence of God that have been put forth and defended by some of the best atheistic thinkers in the world. This can be a dangerous exercise, unless one is committed to the truth. As I have often said, if I am to give my entire being to another being who claims to be the "supreme" being, I personally want to know this being is really "being." (Please read the preceding sentence again, just in case it confused you. It confused me, and I wrote it.)

If believing in this being is just a guess, even if it is a good guess, count me out. Even though many believe Thomas was being a bit weak in faith when he demanded proof that Jesus was really alive (John 20:25), remember that the other apostles had already seen Jesus alive and conversed with him, and Thomas was ready to go and die with Jesus in John 11. Let us also remember that the entire book of John is presenting evidence so we might believe that Jesus is the Christ, the Son of God (John 21:24–25 NIV). Jesus stated, "Anyone who has seen me has seen the Father" (John 14:9 NIV). God is all-wise. He desperately desires that we know him. He spent his life helping us see that he is real.

And now back to the class, and the sneaky professor. We knew the teacher and that he was setting us up. Thus he did. "Well," he began, "did God know before he created this "playground" of the world that there would be intense suffering, disease, injustice, pain, hunger, natural disasters, horrific abuse of children, and ultimately death of everyone? And not only the physical problems, but did he also know that the majority of people would rebel against him, so much so that his heart would be grieved that he made humans?"

I believe that was the moment the real fun began. Here I am in graduate school, where I am attempting to prepare myself to go and preach about a loving God. In one fifteen-minute span of a three-hour class period, I have traveled from being absolutely sure of my career choice and excited about it, to one confused, bewildered, angry not-having-a-clue-what-I-am-going-to-be-when-I-grow-up, twenty-three-year-old. Thanks, Dr. Tawa.

In the ensuing months and even years, those questions kept bouncing around my brain. At least, said my wife years later in a different yet similar context, those bouncing around questions didn't have far to bounce. But bounce they did. So what is the answer?

First, I repeat again that no human can have all the answers to all God questions, for no human invented God. But note this as well: it is all right to search for answers, for if God does exist, and if we were created in his image, then the asking of such questions is as natural as... being confused by them. And there is too much dirt not to wash our hands on occasion.

The following attempt to make some sense of this supposed nonsense is all under the umbrella of attempting to speak right about God. God knows this is the intent. If there are holes in what I am about to propose, that is okay as long as the presenter (me) recognizes that this is an attempt to help us grow in our understanding of the complex, always-existing God.

Then why did God create us, evidently knowing the sin, rebellion, pain, and death to come? We certainly would not have built that playground; he knew the stakes, saw what was coming, and built it anyway.

We have already attempted a beginning response: why do we as parents have children, knowing the pain and sin that is coming to our children if they live long enough? And if they don't, then we have their deaths to deal with. We bring them into this world out of hearts of love (for the most part). Though some decide not to have children because of the pain to come, they have the ability to make such decisions because their parents chose to have children in spite of the pain. Perfect wisdom (God's, not humans') says that existence with a choice to love is better than no existence at all.

God certainly knew the evil to come before he flipped on the switch of creation. Being God, thus being all-wise, this decision must be the right one, though the rightness of it does not always feel right. But if we dare think through this supposed dilemma, the rightness of the decision might just make a bit of sense to us who appear to be senseless at times. And dare I say, when this begins to crystallize in this head of mine, my worth, the worth of living, begins to excite the soul, perhaps for the first time.

God, knowing yet still creating, proves beyond any doubt the exciting possibilities of living. The risk of creating outweighed the alternative not creating. Just the possibility of a relationship between Creator and creature ignited God's senses. Living, even with the real possibility of dying, far outshines never existing. We exist, so states Paul, "for the praise of his glory" (Ephesians 1: 12 NIV).

It is better then to have a chance to love God and be in full fellowship with him than to never exist, never to have the possibility of that experience. Hear C. S. Lewis: "If God thinks this state of war in the universe a price worth paying for free will... then we may take it as worth paying."[11]

The smog of life often blots out the beauty of fresh air and sunlight. At times we have experienced so much pollution that we forget that flowers still bloom and rainbows can still suddenly appear.

O, do not underestimate the wisdom of God or his knowledge of things to come. Before he created one atom, molecule, animal, or human, he heard the abused children screaming for help; he saw the anguished parent who had lost a child, and the grieving widow who buried her husband riddled with dementia. He saw all the pain to come and the wars and rumors of war. His future vision was and is always 20/20.

Yet God gave two thumbs up to Creation in the face of the tears and the pain. Why? Because it is worth it! Having relationships with his creation is what God is all about. It is what we are all about, to experience this relationship with our Creator. Nothing else makes sense. Thus, this relationship must be an amazing experience that transforms everything about living. This concept can and does escape us for a while. We get tastes of it now and then, but it must be worth it because the price paid for just the possibility of this relationship is enormous both for God and for us.

Georg Hegel, a nineteenth-century German philosopher, wrote, "To think of God means to rise above what is sensuous, external, and individual. It means to rise up to what is pure, to that which is unity with itself... it is going... into the pure regions of the universe."[12]

Do we really live like that? Is this "life" for you? Was Jesus merely talking when he boldly stated, "I have come that you might have life to the very fullest" (John 10:10 NIV)? Or might he have had inside information on the meaning of real life?

There is a connected yet somewhat distinct reason that explains God creating—he had to. God, being the source of all there is, is the original source of love. His definition is clearly portrayed in scripture with one word, love. To keep this simple, which is easy for me, love must love. To be described as a person of total, perfect love, and to not love, is a contradiction. Perfect love must love.

We know that God, being three in one, has always loved. The community of the deity, confusing as it is, has one clearly taught theme: God the Father, God the Son, and God the Holy Spirit are one. They love one another. Was this perfect, divine love not enough? Many seem to think so. Then why create others to love, knowing the disastrous consequences to follow? Really, only God knows the answer to that one. But one tweak of our thinking might just help a little. God's love, totally complete and perfect, was forced to create. God might appear to be contradictory at times to finite humans (ask Abraham about that). However, God in truth can never contradict himself.

A teenager once asked me if I thought God could sin. I responded with a resounding "No!" God is holy, and God could not possibly sin; in fact, I added, He could not even desire to sin, for that would go against his very self. This is difficult for me to grasp emotionally, even though I get it intellectually. I am tempted to sin daily, perhaps hourly. Though I really do not desire to sin, every time I do sin, I am stating that I want to sin. I cannot conceive of a time when there is no battle with sin.

God then, in one way of addressing this, could not possibly have chosen not to create. God cannot even think of sinning. He cannot be tempted by evil, nor does he tempt us to sin. It is not that he battles with this decision, as if he might just possibly dare choose to sin. No! He cannot sin, therefore he cannot not love—for not loving is sin; it is against the very self of God. Love must love; thus God, by his love, is forced (by his own being) to create creatures to love and who will hopefully love him back. One question: am I really fulfilling total love if I only love my wife and myself? We are one, as God and the Son and the Spirit are one. If God only loves God, though God is three, that is basically God loving himself. Apparently, to God's way of thinking, that love is not all there is to his love.

John, called the "apostle of love," startles his readers with these words: "No one has ever seen God; but if we love one another, God lives in us and his love is made complete in us" (1 John 4:12 NIV). Could John be hinting that if we (humans) do not exist, God's love is not complete?

My first sermon was based on Matthew 5:43–48. In preparing for that debacle, I decided to read the New Testament until I found something to preach. When I read these words of Jesus about loving our enemies, I was awestruck with the simple yet profound wisdom of his words. "Be perfect therefore as your heavenly father is perfect," he concluded. Oh really? I thought. I am just five chapters into reading the Bible for the first time, and already I am told I must be perfect as God is perfect?

Thus motivated to discover the meaning of these words, I proceeded to re-read the short paragraph. What could he mean by being perfect? The only explanation is that he meant that we must love as God loves. Perfect, complete love includes loving both those that love you and those that do not love you. We become like God and are called "children of God," when we love completely—that is when we love our enemies.

While we were... enemies... God loved us (see Romans 5). So a strong case can be made that without humans, who can choose to love or not to love God, God's love could not possibly be complete; he would love only himself. Perfect love loves regardless of the response of the object of our love. Perfect love continues to love even when the one loved is imperfect. Thus, could we say that the Being who is perfect love needs our very existence, as free-will creatures with the capacity to love and not to love? God must love completely. He needs us to complete his love. He loves the unlovable (us), and he receives love from us, once we accept his love for us. His love always precedes ours (1 John 4:7).

As difficult as this is to write, much less to believe, God seemingly needs something outside of himself to completely, totally love. He does not need it for his existence or to complete something lacking in his character. No, all of this loving others is bound up in his very being. As parents have children who are an extension of their love for each other, so God creates humans as his children, extensions of his perfect love.

Stating that God needs to love sends many scholarly theologians into defense mode. But one thought keeps creeping into this brain of mine when I read such defenses. Where does it state that needing love weakens us, especially when that need comes from the character of God himself?

When I discuss this theory with live audiences, as opposed to dead ones, the feedback is swift and intense. It is as if I have betrayed God. "God can do anything," many shout. Thus he could choose not to create. How dare I state that God has no choice, that somehow he is forced to create?

I understand that thinking. It is what most of us have been taught. But certainly we know better, that there are many things God cannot do. As already noted, he cannot sin, nor can he tempt us to sin (James 1:13). Hebrews tells us God cannot lie. One who is defined as "truth" of course cannot lie. We can lie, thus to even think about a Being who cannot lie, well, appears to be a lie! It is the same with a Being who is defined as "love" (1 John 4:8). That being simply must love.

God created us to love us. He created animals to serve us. Animals, I repeat, no matter how much we love them and need them at times, never discuss these things. Having a relationship with anyone, as we have discussed, benefits both parties. God is benefitted by us because of his love. He "worthifies" us by his love. We are here because of his love. We are created out of his heart of love.

God has a dilemma. We must exist because of his love. For humans to truly love, choice must be an option—the choice not to love. (Here's another paradox about God: "love" defines God. His love is absolute, absolutely pure and perfect. It is so perfect that it appears that he has no choice but to love. Again, the gulf between God and us is clearly seen!).

Any creature (us) created with the image of the creator within them must have the capacity to love. This means we must have choice, and that choice must involve the choice not to love. Once again, C.S. Lewis's words ring true: "If God thinks this state of war in the universe a price worth paying for free will...then we may take it is worth paying."[13]

And that is why we have the mess of the world. Even God cannot create us to always choose to love him, for that is a contradiction. He cannot force us to freely choose. If he forces us, we are not free. If we are truly free, we must have an opportunity to choose to say no to the Creator.

Recently, in one of our retreats we lead for those who have experienced loss, a woman attended whose thirteen-year-old daughter had ended her life by suicide. The mother, of course distraught with grief and guilt and confusion, made a couple of pointed and honest statements to me during a break. "I am so damn angry at God. Where the hell was he when my little girl needed him? Why didn't He stop her from doing this? I used to love God, but now I just do not know if I can ever love God again."

I asked for permission to give my opinion as to where God was during this tragic time leading up to her daughter's death. She gave it, so I proceeded.

"The reason I believe God did not stop your daughter was because He *could not* stop her and at the same moment have her be a free-will human. The price of love is free will. If He stopped her from making free will choices…then she would not be human. And I do believe God weeps with you. And God has done something to stop this death march we all seem to be on in this thing called living."

At this point, the grieving mom interrupted. "But I thought God could do anything. He is God! Therefore He can do all things."

"God can only do what God can do," I responded. "If he stops us every time we are about to make a bad decision, then there is no way we are free, and thus not human. And He knows our stories, and knows the pain your daughter was in. His heart is so touched by your pain now, and he does grieve with you. And God has taken care of this death issue."

I know the preceding can lead to our brain hurting. Mine does not feel so good as I write this. Just think how God must feel. We are here, in this messed up world, because of the heart of God!

Let me be absolutely clear here. Without God being the God of love, we do not exist. We do exist, thus our being is his fault. But that does not blame God for our sin choices. All sin choices are our own fault.

But now hear this, please. No one, as previously discussed, asked to be born into this world. This is all God's doing. All humans, who live long enough, will eventually freely choose to sin. Thus, our entry into this world brings two inevitable possibilities:

1. I will die before I ever freely choose to sin, which means I will die quite young, or I am mentally incapable of deciding right from wrong. If you are in this category, do not worry. For one thing, you are not reading this book, for you are either too young, or you are not mentally capable of deciding right from wrong. So you guys are okay. There is only one possible alternative.

2. I will sin before I die. Since we are obviously still here or I wouldn't be writing this book and you wouldn't be reading it, we need Jesus to rectify the sticky problem God's love started.

The God who created us out of his heart of love, knew the pain coming, the pain to himself, and the pain coming to us. He certainly also realized what all of us know as well: live long enough and the odds that you will sin is one hundred percent. In other words, our entrance into living is actually our death sentence, unless of course the Creator intervenes. It is entirely dependent on him to do something that is impossible for us to do. If you and I have figured this out, the infinite Creator God certainly has also. He knows it and feels it.

The Psalms are filled with insights into God's heart and soul. The poets who wrote many of the psalms seem to somehow know the deep things of God. It is not as if they are writing a theological textbook, but theology is certainly presented. Psalm 103 illustrates this. The writer, David, is overwhelmed with the immensity of God's love. See if, according to David's words, God understands our entrance into this world, and the handicap this emergence into the land of the conscious, breathing humans brings to each of us.

In the first thirteen verses, David praises God for many reasons:

- God's love.
- It is God who redeems us from the pit.
- He crowns us with love and righteousness.
- He satisfies our desires with good things.
- He renews our youth like the eagle's.
- He rescues the oppressed.
- He makes his ways known.
- He is slow to anger, and he abounds in love.
- He will not always accuse.
- His love is as high as the heavens are above the earth.
- He has removed our sins as far as the east is from the west.
- And as a father has compassion on his children, so God has compassion on us.

The thinker who wrote these words apparently wanted to know why God loves like that. What explains the vastness and the steadfastness and the tenacity of his love? Verse fourteen tells us why. We might miss it unless we stop and consider each word. "For He knows how we are formed, He remembers that we are dust" (Psalm 103:14 NIV).

Father God, just how were we formed? Who formed us? Who made us like the dust that we are here one moment, and by the mere blowing of the wind, we are gone the next moment? Who understands, O God, what we were born into when we came into this world? And God, who is ultimately responsible?

"I am responsible!" God admits.

The Creator knows the creation. The One who spoke us into existence knows the pitfalls that come with being human. And he knows the only one who is capable of making a difference. He realizes that he alone must do all that he can to redeem us out of this pit. He alone created us. The all-loving God is once again compelled by his love. He creates us because he and only he is love. He never stops loving us and attempting to redeem us because He is love. And since he is ultimately responsible for us and for our predicament, he must do all he can to rescue us. And so he has.

Three = One

> In the beginning was the Word, and the Word was with God, and the Word was God.
>
> John 1:1 (NIV)

The concept called the Trinity was actually coined by Tertullian, sometime in the second century A.D. The easiest way to describe the Trinity is that God is three persons but only one God. Though the word *trinity* is not found in scripture, the concept of God being three in one is taught clearly and often. Jesus himself, who should have known, and he did know, believed it so decisively that he stated it as true as if he were talking about 2 + 2 = 4. After all, he had a long time to get used to the three-being-one equation.

If you accept scripture as the absolute authority in such matters, then you, too, believe that God is three in one. Of course, this does not mean we understand it or that we can explain it.

Google the word *trinity* and you can easily find all the scriptures that support this concept. The baptism of Jesus by John is one of the scriptures that lends credence to the truth of the trinity concept. Jesus was baptized, the Spirit descended on him as a dove, and the voice of the Father boomed out of heaven, claiming that Jesus was God's Son. John claims in John 1:1 that the Word was with God, and in fact *was* God, and "both" (one?) were from the beginning. This "Word" became flesh (Jesus) and made his dwelling among us (John 1:14 NIV).

Jesus said in John 8:58 that "Before Abraham was born, I am," claiming to be God himself, yet God was also residing separately from him. He was born as the Son of Man (human) and the Son of God, with Mary giving birth to a baby who was conceived by the Holy Spirit of God the Father.

In John 14–17, Jesus equates the Spirit and the Father with himself, as all three reside in one another and in fact within us as well (more about that later). Actually, if one was debating within oneself as to the logic of the existence of God, this one discussion of the Trinity could be the clinching argument to both believe in God and disbelieve in God, almost at the same moment.

When we (or I should say I?) think about the Trinity, I know with almost absolute certainty that God therefore could not exist; yet within about 4.5 seconds, the thinking turns to an astounding "Aha!" because the Trinity concept proves the exact opposite. God *must* exist, and the three-in-one concept must be true for him to exist. Instead of rejecting the idea of God because of the Trinity, I believe in God even more dogmatically *because* of it.

God must be singular. He is the uncaused cause, the source of all there is. His existence is unlike any other existing thing, for he is the only non-contingent being. There can be only one being from whom all else comes. He has always existed. All other things have not always been here. There can be only one source of all there is. God must be one.

God must be plural. God is love. That is his basic definition. He is perfect in love, and thus God must always love. Who would God love before Creation if God were one? Is it really perfect love to love nothing? I have postulated that creation of humans with the capacity to love and be loved flows out of the loving heart of God—that God's nature, in a sense, forces him to create.

The three-in-one concept makes sense in the context of love. God must be plural.

There are other considerations that make sense of these two apparent contradictory statements that God must be singular, and God must be plural. God's love, which leads to the creation of humans, presents God with the classic dilemma: what does God do with those he loves when they freely choose sin, which is the exact opposite of God and his holiness? Feeling the responsibility, God realizes that he alone is responsible to redeem fallen humans. So before the creation of the world, God decided on Plan A, and he realized that there was no Plan B. God must become human and pay the price for all our sins, and God must die.

Do not underestimate the enormity of the problem God's coming to earth and his death presented to God himself, especially if God was only singular. If God had just been one person, then his death would have spelled death to us all. There would have been no God to run the store. If God were one, who would have strengthened Jesus while he was on the earth? Who would have protected him through all the preliminary attempts to kill him? I suppose Jesus never would have made it to the cross had there been no one at home in heaven.

The Father would not exist without the Son, and the Son would not exist without the Father. The same is true of the Spirit. God the Father cannot exist without his Spirit. And the Son understands his place in all this as well. In addition, the plan for God to save us from sin necessitated all three persons of God to work together to bring it about. Thus, God must be three in one. And he must be but one God.

I realize this thinking can drive us all completely mad. In presenting this material at our church recently (the material about the Trinity), a man came up to me when class was over and told me his brain was hurting. He asked for a couple of extra-strength Tylenol. I replied that I didn't have any because I had taken my last four just before class began.

One more side point: if my friend Jim and I decided to fool the world and make up a story about there being an uncaused first cause called God, I doubt if we would have come up with a one-but-three concept of God.

God Doing All He Can

> He who did not spare his own Son, but gave him up for us all—how will He not also, along with him graciously give us all things?
>
> Romans 8:32 (NIV)

Do you agree or disagree with the following? "If God *could* save one more person from Hell, and does not, then he is not all-loving." Or this one: "If there is something more God *could* do to save us, and he does not do it, then he is not all-loving." And the inevitable conclusion, at least from my way of thinking: "If God *could* do more to save us and doesn't, then he is not the God I desire to serve."

My mother was born and raised in New Zealand. Many years ago, we visited the land of her birth, and we met many relatives we had never seen before, and may never see again. One night, many of us sat down for a lovely dinner of lamb chops and all the trimmings. Seated at the table was one of my aunts, who knew I was a preacher, and one of her sons-in-law, whom she knew was an atheist.

This aunt of mine was a strong believer in God and seized this opportunity to make her statement through me. I had no clue what she was about to do. If I had, I am sure I would have gladly eaten ivy with the little lambs instead of eating the little lambs.

"Everyone, this is David, Valerie's youngest son. He is a preacher. And this is Jon, my son-in-law, and he is an atheist. Now you two talk, and we all will listen."

My first thought was: *Now isn't this special?*

So of course we all just sat there awkwardly. It seemed that minutes passed before I broke the silence. For some reason, when I am put on the spot by a relative from New Zealand, I feel this huge responsibility to do something. Strangely, I am not like that at home, unless the relative has made the trip to see me.

So I began, "So, Jon, Paddy says you are an atheist. How interesting. And by the way, welcome to the family."

"Thank you, Dave. Or should I call you Right Reverend or something of that sort, mate?"

"Not necessary, mate. Last I checked I am left-handed, even though some say I am ambidextrous. But as I always remind them, I would give my right arm to be ambidextrous."

I believe it was at that point that my astute wife kicked me under the table, twice. That is our signal that I am saying things totally out of line, that my humor is failing terribly, and that I, being from Texas, do not have to use the word *mate* when talking to someone from "down under."

"Sorry for the poor attempt at humor, Jon. Just call me Dave or David if you prefer. Can you share with me exactly why you have chosen to be an atheist? And by the way, you should feel honored. You are the very first genuine, authentic, self-admitted atheist I have ever met."

Jon looked as shocked as I felt after the introductions by Paddy, and by the way, he did not get my humor (or is that *humour*)? "Glad to oblige, mate. My real hang-up is the whole idea of suffering and hell. If God created all things, then he must have known the pain and suffering to come. He also must have created hell. That simply makes no sense. Why doesn't he stop the suffering and simply eliminate hell? Is your God sadistic? If he exits, there should not be such suffering in this world and certainly not a thing called hell. If God is all-powerful, as you Christians claim, and if he is all-good, then God would want to eliminate evil and suffering, and he certainly could do that. So since evil and suffering most certainly exist, then your God could not exist."

"So suffering and hell are God's fault?"

"Of course they are. What other explanation can you give? How do you live knowing that your God willingly let's millions be born into outrageous situations, then sends millions to hell to be tortured forever, when he doesn't have to do that. I simply cannot believe in a being so vicious."

"I totally agree with you," I began. "The God I serve is not like that. Perhaps this will make more sense. If God exists, then we must exist, for he is a God of perfect love. He hates the suffering more than we do. Our free choice has led to this fallen world. And speaking of hell, well, it must exist if God exists. Hell is the place where God is not. God hates hell worse than you do. He has done everything he can possibly do to keep you and all the rest of us out of hell. Hell is a consequence of God's existing, not really a choice of God, as we view choice."

We discussed other things, such as how God's existence leads to our existence, which leads to our free choice, which leads to sin and, thus, God's problem, and the like. He said he would think about it, that the explanation that this world and hell is a consequence of God's existence and not his choice, had softened him a bit, and that he was a little more open to the idea of God than before.

THE GOD WHO CANNOT DO EVERYTHING

The concept that God cannot do everything puzzles traditional believers in God. After all, scripture, the basis of many believers' faith in God, states clearly that all things are possible with God; that God indeed can do everything. Once, in discussing the idea that God cannot do everything with a class of college students, one extremely bright senior not only disagreed with me, but also almost wrote me off as a complete infidel, challenging my very personhood. I truly felt as if he thought I had somehow forfeited not only my position as the preacher but also my very existence as a human being.

When scripture claims that "with God all things are possible" (Matthew 19:26), obviously the context deserves to be considered. Scripture also states that God cannot sin, cannot lie, and cannot tempt us to sin. The Bible tells us that God desires that all of us be saved while also claiming that all will *not* be saved. So here is another thing God apparently cannot do: he cannot save all people, even though he desires to do so.

My friend, when hearing this defense of my position, stated confidently that God could indeed sin if he so desired. He simply chose not to sin, but that if he wanted to sin, then who are we to say that he cannot sin? I respect his right to have an opinion, but defer to the scripture that states that God "cannot" sin. Again, I can sin. To think of a being that cannot sin is almost beyond my ability. The God who could sin would not be the God. He would only be a god.

My friend also affirmed that God could save everyone, if he chose to do so, and he could stop all suffering on this earth if he desired. I would add that my friend would also say that God could take away all bad choices and somehow make us always freely choose to do the right thing. I responded with 2 Peter 3:9 that says God is "not wanting anyone to perish, but everyone to come to repentance." If God could save everyone, then why would he not save everyone? If he *can* but *doesn't*, then evidently he certainly does not have the desire to save everyone.

There are other things God apparently cannot do either. God cannot save anyone without the death and resurrection of Jesus. Presenting this thought is almost as dangerous as the others mentioned above. The thinking again goes back to the mistaken definition of *omnipotence*, or *all-powerful*. Many assume that these terms mean God can do everything. Jon, my atheist relative, rejected the entire concept of God on this basis. "Your God can do everything, thus he could eliminate suffering and hell and have everyone lead a perfect, happy life. Since we have suffering, and hell is clearly taught as being real, then God is not a god of love. Your concept of this God is absurd. It just does not compute."

If this God could have saved us all without Jesus dying, then he made his only Son suffer and die when it was not absolutely necessary! What kind of God is that?

If God *can* save someone, yet simply refuses, then how does this fit with the scripture that says he "is not wanting anyone to perish?" (2 Peter 3:9).

God loves the world, everyone in the world. His intense desire is for each person to be with him forever. If he could save everyone, no matter what his or her free choice does, he most certainly would save everyone. The only conclusion is: God has done and will do everything he can possibly do to pursue us and eventually to save us.

Most people with whom I have discussed this have a hard time understanding the relevancy of it all. "What difference does it make?" they ask. "Just believe; don't trouble me with all these questions."

I believe it does make a difference—a huge difference! Innocent children by the millions through the ages have endured intense suffering, and it somehow is not necessary? That God could stop it if he so desired, but he does not stop or prevent it? Billions upon billions going to hell forever, and God could save them, but because he is God, he can and evidently *chooses not* to save them? I will say this often: I am not, and I will not give my heart to that god. Since the intense suffering continues as I write these words, if the above is true, the only conclusion is that God does not desire to stop it. That is not the God I serve and love.

Any being who is all-powerful can only do what an all-powerful being can do. I know that is another profound statement. But *all-powerful* does not mean that being can do that which is contradictory. Two + two = four... always. Even an all-powerful being would be graded wrong on a test if the being put "five" down as the answer.

God can do only what he can do. He cannot go against his own self. Perfect holiness cannot be unholy. Absolute truth cannot be false. All-wise has no way of being foolish. Even God cannot know that which is never to be. (For instance, God cannot know that a year from now my dad will go to Disney World for many reasons. First, because Dad would never go to Disney World. Second, because Dad has been dead since 1993.)

Once a professor asked his class if God could make someone five foot two and six foot two at the same time. Or could he make a square circle? Of course he cannot. God could not possibly make my triplet daughters go to college or anything else for that matter simply because I do not *have* triplet daughters. That is impossible even for an all-powerful being. It is not as if adding power to God would give him enough power to make someone two different heights at the same time or to make a square circle. It is akin to asking the question, "Can God make a rock so big that he cannot lift it?" The only answer is: of course he can, and of course he cannot.

All of this apparently ridiculous discussion has a vital point: God, even the all-powerful, all-knowing, infinite God of the universe, cannot do everything. He is indeed limited by his very being and by his creation, which is you and me.

Let me summarize with this: God is love. Love must love, which resulted in God creating humans with the capacity to love and love him back. Love demands a free choice. Free choice means the possibility and the reality that humans will eventually say no to the Creator. God is ultimately responsible for our *being* and feels compelled by his love, not by any weakness, to provide a way out for us. The free choice that he gave us means that many will freely choose to accept God's way out. It also means that many will freely choose to reject that way out. That hell is a natural consequence of who God is, and not a choice of God as we normally think.

God's radical action, his unbelievable response to all of this, proves without question that the above is true. God knows better than all of us that he is the only one capable of a solution to the mess of the world. There is nothing greater that God could do to rectify this mess. If anyone can think of something greater, then please let it be known. My guess is that your idea would pale when compared to the greatest story ever told. The infinite God willingly sacrificed his only Son, who willingly agreed to undergo the greatest suffering possible, so that we might get out of the mess of our sins.

The Ugliest, Worst Human Ever

> The servant grew up before God—a scrawny seedling, a scrubby plant in a parched field. There was nothing attractive about him, nothing to cause us to take a second look. He was looked down on and passed over, a man who suffered, who knew pain firsthand. One look at him and people turned away. We looked down on him, thought he was scum.
>
> Isaiah 53:1-3 (The Message)

Who, in your opinion, is the worst person who has lived or is living in the world? Who is the ugliest? What would be the criteria for determining these? And why do I ask these questions? I have one person in mind that fits both categories—he was the worst person, and he was some kind of ugly.

I doubt if anyone could be born who would out-worst him or out-ugly him. If we really knew the truth, we would all agree with this: he was the ugliest human. He was full of sin. Undoubtedly he was the world's greatest sinner. Sin turns one ugly—some kind of ugly.

He felt the guilt of every sin ever committed, from Eve's many years ago to yours or mine a few seconds ago. If one could combine all the sins every human has committed throughout the ages and add them up to one gigantic number, then we might get a little closer to the amount of sin he felt. But we would still fall short of true understanding.

Name all the sins of the world you can imagine, starting with the worst. At the top of my list would be those sins I would never consider doing, such as harming innocent children, abusing them, beating them, abandoning them, using them for my own profit and pleasure. Throw in betrayal, murder, cheating, lying, and using others for my own gain. He was guilty of every sin on the list, guilty even of sins you cannot name. Think of the sins you personally have never committed, would never think about doing, even those sins that repulse you. He felt the sting of each of them. Amazingly, he was not in any kind of denial. He freely chose to take on all of these sins.

He was so ugly that the face of his own Father was turned away. The Father could not look upon the face of his only Son. That must have been one ugly human!

You know his name, yet you might feel uncomfortable saying his name after that description. You might even be angry or at least a bit disturbed at me for linking the ugliest human, the worst human ever, to that name.

"He had no beauty or majesty to attract us to him, nothing in his appearance that we should desire him" (Isaiah 53:2 NIV). He was ugly.

He was "like one whom men hide their faces" (v. 3). He was brutally ugly.

The Lord laid on him every single one of our sins. "He was numbered with the transgressors" (v. 12). He was one ugly, sin-stenched (by our sins), human.

I am sitting by a pool in Skagway, Alaska, on a cruise ship. Today, I did something I rarely do: I put on a bathing suit, took off my shirt, and got in a pool in public. The reason I rarely do this, quite frankly, is my body. Years ago when puberty hit me, it brought along pimples and acne so severe that my chest and back were left scarred. At times, when few are around, I take the risk and jump in the pool.

It is May, and here in Alaska the sun is shining and suddenly it is seventy-five degrees. My wife and I got into the pool before the other cruisers realized what a grand day it is. Now, as I write these words, the pool is filled. I am safe though. The shirt is back on, and no scars are showing.

My scars have remained for some forty-five years now. Not long ago, I was preaching on Jesus being the worst sinner, though he actually never sinned. The verse from Isaiah kept coming up. He was wounded for our sins, he was bruised for our iniquity; by his stripes we are healed. He took on my scarring for my sins. He became the ugly one.

I have felt ugly all my life, at least once the scars came. It used to make me angry at the world for leaving me behind and angry with God for giving me this ugly body.

But this I now know: I am not the ugliest human any longer. Jesus is. He has more scars than I do. In fact, I have no scars remaining—the last time I checked, the *real* scars are gone. I kind of like my physical blemishes now (almost). They remind me that my real scars are gone forever.

I know what it is like to feel ugly. Do you? This weekend I attended the fortieth reunion of my high school church youth group. They showed pictures of us from 1969 and 1970. There were a couple of pictures of me. I cried later that night in my room. My wife asked me what was wrong, because I could not hold back the tears. I explained that the pictures brought back those days when I felt ugly. I saw pain and loneliness in those eyes of forty years ago. But then I remembered what I had been preaching: I am not the ugliest person any longer, Jesus is. I am actually quite the handsome one. My real scars are gone!

I am stunned by Jesus! I cannot explain him away. The most beautiful willingly became the most ugly. The one who knew no sin became sin. The pure and holy became the despised and the wicked. And the face of the Father was turned away. Holy, holy. holy, had become sinful, sinful, sinful.

I often wonder what it was like having your own Father turning away from his only Son, especially when the only Son was simply being obedient to the Father he loved so much.

Last week, a man in his fifties came to see me. His life reeked of disaster. His wife despised him; his kids ignored him, effectively banning him from their lives, and the lives of his four grandchildren. Pathetic was his own word to describe his condition.

I felt immense sadness for him, and I sensed a heavy darkness engulfing him.

"Tell me your story," I said. Everyone has a story.

So he did. He was six when his father left the family for good. His mother was a drug addict with apparently no desire to get help. Three younger siblings would now depend on this six-year-old for protection, provision, and guidance. The father hugged his youngest children, telling them how much he loved them. Not so with the six-year-old. All he received from dear old Dad was a weak handshake and a stern rebuke when Jon began to tear up. Not a word of love or encouragement from Dad came that day, or for any day in the future. Jon's father turned his face from him, and Jon has never been whole again.

Recently, a friend of mine came to see me. Bob is an interesting person. His I.Q. dwarfs mine. Other friends say that it is no big deal. He teaches a subject matter, that I cannot even spell, at a state university. His dissertation might confuse Albert Einstein. Our meeting was more of a counseling session than a friendly chat over coffee. Earlier his wife had informed me that she was leaving Bob after thirty-five years of marriage. He had not shown any affection in all those years, never once coming close. She felt dishonored, disrespected, and unloved, and she could not take it for another day.

After many hours of counseling over a period of a few weeks, one day the emotional dam broke. Bob remembered something he had tucked away for forty years. His father, his one and only father, had sexually abused Bob beginning when Bob was eight years old. Bob had never told anyone this dark secret, because he had so repressed it, that even he didn't remember until the day he told me.

Bob's mother and dad were leaders in their community. Everyone thought they were the model couple and family. Bob only did what his father told him to do. A dutiful son. Yet when, at the age of eleven, Bob told his father no, all hell broke loose. His mom defended her husband; his dad said Bob was delusional.

Ask Bob what it is like to try to be a dutiful son, and then experience total rejection from the two who should love you no matter what. *If my own parents despise me...*

Now, back to Jesus.

Let me see if I understand this. "Son, go do this, and when you do, I can't have anything to do with you for a while." Right. That makes a lot of sense.

But it does. The righteous for the unrighteous. The truth for a liar. The holy for the sexually deviant. The life-giver for all the murderers. It all makes sense now.

Do not think for a moment that God could have saved us in any other way. If he could have, there would be no scars on his only Son. That would be cruel and sadistic, if there were another way.

He was some kind of ugly.

The Disappearance of God

> The incarnation is a kind of vast joke whereby the Creator of the ends of the earth comes among us in diapers... Until we too have taken the idea of the God-man seriously enough to be scandalized by it, we have not taken it as seriously as it demands to be taken.
>
> —Frederick Buechner

To understand a little better the enormity of the sacrifice of Jesus and the love of the Father for us, we somehow need to get into the mind of Jesus and the mind of God the Father. This could be the real *Mission Impossible.* However, scripture indicates it might be just what we were made to do. We are to have the mind of Christ (Philippians 2:5). Peter, the fallen coward, claims later that we, including you and me and all who have ever lived on this earth, can participate in the divine nature (2 Peter 1:4 NIV). Now I am getting a little excited. Again I say, we cannot totally "get" God in this fallen world, but we certainly can grow in our understanding, appreciation, and adoration for him.

Years ago, I was teaching a parenting class with about fifty couples. Each week we had an assignment that we were to complete and then report on the following week. One week the assignment appeared simple: spend fifteen minutes a day alone with each child. We had three children at the time, so I was committing forty-five minutes a day to be able to set the right example for the class, my being the teacher and all.

Our oldest was six at the time. His youngest sister had just entered the world. We were together, alone, just before bedtime. Looking back, I now see that this can be a deadly combination for young (or old) parents. He asked two questions that night that staggered me. You might not think that the questions are all that tough. But two experiences recently had made the answering of those questions problematic.

First, I had recently coached his mother (for the third time) in the "Let's have a baby without any pain medicine" game. Most parents are familiar with the process—cleansing breaths, focal points, counting. For the life of me, I saw nothing wrong with giving something to the *father* to help ease the anxiety. By the time the third little rascal was born, I would gladly have taken the famed saddle block, and I don't even ride horses.

Second, the questions he asked that fateful night had never been asked to me in all my thirty-five years of living; and to my relief have never been asked again.

The first question: "Daddy, did Jesus just disappear?" I had no idea what this kid of mine was thinking. Did he think he saw a vision of Jesus in his room? Was he referring to some Bible story I had somehow never read?

"What do you mean, Adam?"

"Did Jesus disappear? You know, he was with God, and then he became a baby in his mommy's tummy. You've heard that story, haven't you, Daddy?"

Yes, I suppose I had heard that story a time or two. But in all the years of teaching Bible classes, no one had come close to asking that question.

"Dad, you see, Jesus was with God all the time in heaven before he became a baby, right?"

"Yes, I would say that is basically correct, son. Continue please, Adam." (At that point, I hurriedly secured pen and paper and proceeded to take copious notes. I had a sermon to preach the next Sunday.)

"So when Mary got pregnant, what happened to Jesus in heaven? He could not have been in heaven and in Mary at the same time, could he, Daddy?"

Honestly, I had never thought about it. What did happen to him? What was it like to be with eternal God, to be the *logos*, to be God (John 1:1) in one moment, and then to be a fetus in a peasant woman the next? There had to be some point when the *logos* was with God, and then was in the form of a human named Jesus in the next moment.

What was it like in heaven at that moment? One minute, total unbroken fellowship of Father, Son, and Spirit. The next second, separation, and in a place no one could imagine? Even if you are not God, even if you are... you! One moment you are enjoying a nice meal with the wife and children, laughing, talking, and then... you're a baby?

How did the two (God and the Holy Spirit) left behind at home feel? Did they miss the Son? Was there an empty place at the divine dinner table? Were their conversations different, incomplete? Did God the Father or the Holy Spirit catch themselves asking the Son his opinion on a given topic, only to realize that he was not there—not there with them as he had been from the beginning? Were their hearts breaking?

And do such questions bother you, or seem a bit trivial? *What does it really matter?* you might be thinking.

I believe it does matter. I want to go "hard after God," as Tozer suggested. I am weary of my weak faith and shallow love and wimpy responses to this incredible love of God. I am agitated that at times I have treated God as a non-being, with little if any resemblance to humans. It is disheartening to see God's people accept a Satan-led attack on the human spirit, convincing so many that they can never measure up, that their past condemns them, and that they are doomed to a life of mediocrity and ultimately failure.

It pains me to see so many marriages end up in the give-up pile, the one relationship on earth God created to imitate the relationship he so desires with us. This special relationship has been so abused and misunderstood and neglected; yet it is the relationship that should revive and exhilarate the human spirit. So often marriage leaves one or both spouses bitter, angry, and alone. It is disturbing to see people, created with God's spark all over them, accept mediocrity as the normal way of life.

It is disturbing to see immense suffering suck the life out of so many. And though some turn their anchors into sails, so many others seem to give up hope and, thus, give up on God. If only we could see and feel his immense and tenacious love for us. If somehow we could catch a glimpse of what he went through when the *Logos* left heaven and came to this earth. For the first time in their existence, which was eternity, Father and Son were apart. There was an empty bedroom in the house and an empty chair at the dinner table. And their long-distance bill must have been enormous.

So, "Did Jesus just disappear?" I guess he did. But the key is this: he *reappeared* on this earth, in human form, proving without doubt his immense love for us and our immense importance to God.

Oh, the second question he asked that night: "Daddy, how did Jesus get into Mary, and how did Kelly get into Mommy?" Now that's one for which I wish I had a good answer.

Knowing the Unknowable

"THE GARDEN OF EDEN JR."

> It's a rather surreal experience, a surrender of the senses to sights, sounds and scents meticulously calculated to bombard you with beauty.
>
> —Steve Whysall, *Vancouver Sun*

Pits traditionally are to be avoided; at least falling into them should be avoided. I know of no one who awakes early, enthusiastically gets out of bed and yells, "Yes! Today I get to fall into a pit."

If pits are to be avoided, then why do so many, including me, seem to spend a lot of time there? And why do we tend to stay there? I am weary of my pit. I do not even like your pit. It is not where I desire to spend the rest of my life.

Today, I confidently, yet humbly proclaim that I am now out of my pit, never to return again. And I want to encourage you to either get out of your pit, or believe that you are at this moment already out of it.

How sad to have the winning Lotto number and not realize it and never cash it in. It is not only tragic for the holder of the ticket, but it's not so great for others who know him or her either. If my sister had the winning ticket for $100 million and never knew it, I would be out at least a million or two. I think she loves me that much.

Getting out of my pit was so easy. Believing I had escaped it somehow escaped me. I now am confident that I have been free from the pit for forty-one years; I have known it for only a few.

Adam and Eve were in the garden, the place God created for them. They had everything they needed for total happiness. Last night my wife and I spent a couple of hours at Butchart Gardens in Victoria Island in Canada. After gasping and oohing and ahhing and snapping 484 pictures, I commented that it should be named Garden of Eden Jr. I am guessing the original Garden of Eden was more beautiful than Junior. How this could be possible is beyond me. I must accept by faith that the garden pre-Fall is more beautiful than any garden post-Fall.

My human brain is telling me I might just be happy living at Butchart Gardens, even in this fallen world. Take away all sin and disease and death, and let me live there, then I know I would be happy. But not Adam and Eve. What happened to their bliss and ultimately to ours? Their thinking became clouded. They listened to the lies of the evil one, and began to doubt. They had the winning Lotto number, but they didn't realize it. Satan's beginning strategy with them proved so successful that he unleashes the same destructive lies on us to this day. The lie?

"God really doesn't love you. He is totally selfish. He does not want you to realize that you and he are so similar. So don't listen to him. Listen to me, and I can get you out of this mess."

When I was in the pit, or at least thought I was, logic often left me, as it did Adam and Eve. God did not put me in the pit. It was my sins, failures, poor choices, and selfishness that slung me into the pit. I believe I am somewhat an intelligent being; others' opinion are not really important. But here's what I surmised for years: I have to plan and strategize to get out of this hole. I must be good enough, long enough to somehow barely escape this pit. I have listened to the tape that ends, "If you choose to accept this mission..." and bought into the thinking that this life is indeed *Mission Impossible.*

How I wish someone had told me years ago what should have been obvious: if my "badness" is the reason I am so deep in this pit, my "goodness" cannot get me out of it, for the badness seems to always be lurking.

Looking back, someone did try, again and again, to tell me that very thing. His name was and still is Jesus.

Paul describes the possibility of the impossible—to know the love that surpasses knowledge (Ephesians 3:19 NIV). He appears obsessed with the one main thought of God's incomparable love for each of us. His prayer for us was that we understand that love, that we *know* the love, which he adds surpasses knowledge.

That has confused me, and I suppose many others. How can we know that which cannot be known? The answer must then border on the impossible. For humans, such as you and me, to know that which is impossible to know would take something extraordinary to help us know it!

That something is the cross.

But the cross out of context is simply a neat yet gory story at its best. But taken in context, the cross shatters impossible. The unknowable becomes knowable. He takes ownership of all my scars, ugliness, failures, and sins.

It is one thing for one who sins to take the punishment for my sins. That in itself is good and powerful and makes for a great story. But for the sinless to willingly take the punishment, now that story is becoming not just a great story, but one for the ages, an incomparable story.

Jesus said and did really strange things. He hung out with really strange people. His life was a paradox, from the first day right to the end.

He was humble with a humility few, if any, possessed. Yet his confidence and boldness were explosive, in more ways than one.

He claimed immortality and was quite a name-dropper. "Moses talked of me," he once boasted. "Abraham? Yes, a good guy, of course. But before Abraham was born, I am. And God? Yes, I know him. In fact, I know him better than anyone else alive, or dead for that matter. I have been there and done that, and I will do it again, but even better. And when I do it again, you will be there with me. I will make sure of that."

Jesus came to be a king, yet when they elected him king, he refused to be sworn in (John 6:15). He came to show everyone who he was, yet often he said to those he healed to tell no one. Jesus never sinned. God cannot sin. Yet Jesus could have sinned, because he was tempted. God cannot be tempted. Jesus, God in the flesh, was tempted.

Jesus, the sinless One who came because of sin, became sin.

Jesus, who hated sin, embraced sin, taking it right between the eyes. The holy of holy One became the world's worst sinner. Jesus, beautiful and righteous and gracious and smiling and lover of little children, Jesus the beautiful and wonderful one, was ugly to the very core of his being, for at least a few hours.

Jesus became sin, scripture proclaims. He thus became everything he was not and all that he detested. Jesus became the greatest living contradiction. Jesus, the eternal logos, died. If God dies, there is no hope for any of us. Yet, Jesus, being God, died to give hope to all of us for the first time.

Jesus, the logos, the very expression of God, expressed God by dying. The Son's dying expresses God, the Giver of Life, mightily. The word *paradox* is not adequate to describe the enormity of the paradox.

When I die, I want those I love, especially my wife and children, to know one thing: I loved them. The One who is defined as "love" created me. I am not God, but I was created by God to be like God.

God, the scriptures say, delights in us. His spark is in each of us. His desire is to love us. How sad for a child to be deeply loved by his daddy but never know it!

A loving couple adopted my wife at birth. Recently, after finding her birth mother and two sisters and older brother, she received a phone call from a woman who was one hundred years old. She knew both of Debbie's adopted parents and her birth mother. She was there when all of those events happened. Her words brought tears to both Debbie and me.

> Your birth grandfather lived close to your house. He worked with your adopted father. Often, he would go visit you and your parents, bringing vegetables he grew in his garden. He absolutely adored you. It broke his heart that he could not tell you the truth, that he was your grandfather.

For over fifty years, Debbie did not know she had a grandfather who adored her. She had feelings of abandonment and some kind of a "disconnect," as do many who are adopted. She now has that different "look" about her, as we discussed in "The Look of Life" chapter. Her grandfather adored her!

God deeply and passionately desires that we, his children, know that he adores us too. It breaks his heart when we do not know that. But when we do accept it and see it, our "look" will change also.

His love is a love that is so incomprehensible that it is described as unknowable. Yet we can indeed know that which we cannot know. It just took the craziest story ever conceived to break our ignorance.

The No-Sin Zone

For the joy set before him he endured the cross.

Hebrews 12:2 (NIV)

The debate has raged for ages. Could Jesus have pulled the trigger and sinned? Second Corinthians 5:21 states confidently that "God made him who had no sin to be sin for us." How did Jesus, fully man, always decide not to sin? If he was fully man, he was surely tempted to sin (Hebrews 4:15). Does not temptation include the necessity of the possibility of sin actually occurring?

Jesus knew no sin. He was not acquainted with sin, nor was he intimate with sin. He did not know what it was like to feel guilt for sin. He never knew any shame.

Jesus became sin. Has anyone else fallen so far and so low? Does anyone else in the world come close to being qualified to *become* sin? Only the holiest of the holy could become the vilest of the vile. If I become utterly sinful, then that is evil, to be sure. Yet I am weak, prone to sin; I am finite, created. I am not the uncaused cause who defines goodness and morality. He is. My middle name is not Truth or Love or Holiness. These words are his first, middle, and last names.

Only he could become everything sin stands for, which is the exact opposite of God himself. Jesus, and no one else, lived each day with no death words, thoughts, actions, or even non-actions.

He was life. He was light. His light was the only true light, so true that his light overcame all darkness and brought true light to every one in the world.

Total, pure life became absolute darkness and total death. Thus, that and that alone is total absolute sin—sin at its lowest form. When God dies, all die. "He became sin " says more than we can comprehend. "He became sin" shouts such outrageous claims that the only conclusion is that it must be true.

To say that Jesus, the only son of the Holy Father, the logos of God, the One who had been from the very beginning, became sin is simply incomprehensible. It is impossible. But it is true.

If Jesus could not have sinned, then he could not have really been tempted. Could one who could not sin really become sin for us? We know he could have sinned from his own words: "Do you not know that I can call down twelve legions of angels..." he said as he made his way to the cross. He did not have to die. Dying was a free-will choice that Jesus made (John 10:11). The father desired him to die. He would have sinned by not dying, for he would have not done the Father's will.

Even if you want to argue that somehow Jesus would have avoided sin even had he chosen not to die on the cross, other instances in his life show us that he was so human that along with that humanness came the opportunity to sin. "How long shall I put up with you?" he asked his apostles in Mark 9:19. Did he not know the answer to his own question? Of course he did. "I have come to die," he shouted in John 12:27, "Shall I say Father save me from this hour?" He knew, didn't he, that he was going to put up with his disciples as long as he had to, which was through the cross? He insisted that he must go to Jerusalem, suffer and die, and then be raised (see Luke 24:46).

The evidence is convincing. Jesus could have sinned; he was tempted to quit on the apostles, to quit on us as well. His desire to be with the Father is understandable. That yearning to be with God, the way he was in the beginning, led to both his temptation to sin (by returning early to the Father) and his resolve not to sin. Another paradox.

For a couple of years, a group of college students, mostly male, gathered in our den on Thursday nights. We talked for hours each week about God and our search for God. There was no agenda, except to be honest and respectful and open with our thoughts and questions. No one would be labeled a heretic or anything worse if they questioned cherished traditions or long-held beliefs.

Inevitably the discussions each week appeared to go back to sex. Imagine that! Here are these unmarried eighteen-to twenty-one-year-olds who all had a passion for God... and other passions as well. Their struggle to be holy is common to all who would be honest. The big questions seemed to center on Jesus and his sinlessness:

- Was Jesus tempted sexually?
- Was he tempted as I am being tempted?
- Did he ever look at a woman and like what he saw?
- Since I believe he was sinless, how did Jesus say no to sin every time?
- We are to be like Jesus; in fact, we are commanded to be like Jesus. But how is that fair?
- If Jesus never sinned, he was not built as I am. He must have had some kind of advantage over me. If no one has made it without sin in the history of the world, how did *he* live without ever sinning?

Those are fair questions. Did God put the protective bubble wrap around him so he could not sin? If so, please do not tell me

I can be like him if I do not get the bonus of the bubble wrap. If he received no special privileges, then how did he do it?

I do not want to even hint that I have all the answers to the dilemma of making sense of this. But I do believe the following helps a little; at least it helps me to get a better grasp on all of it. The following thoughts also motivate me along many lines.

First, let me repeat that the complexities of God prohibit any human on this earth from ever understanding all of him. His mind operates from a radically different plane than ours. As stated earlier, I cannot fathom a no-sin zone, but God can. I truly do not quite grasp a no-time zone either. Imagining eternity with no seasons, beginnings, or endings makes my brain hurt.

Jesus did have one advantage over us: he was with the Father from the beginning. We know from scripture that at some point in his life he had conscious memory of life before incarnation, before he became flesh. No one knows when this might have occurred, of course. We also do not know how much he remembered, whether he remembered in color, or recalled all the details. But this we do know: "For the joy set before him, he endured the cross" (Hebrews 12:2 NIV). "And now, Father, glorify me in your presence with the glory I had with you before the world began" (John 17:5 NIV).

The question remains: how did Jesus stay sinless in the face of real temptation? How could a human, with flesh and blood like ours, who was tempted in every way as we have been and will be tempted, say no every time? What advantage did he have over us? The only one I can think of, which makes at least a little sense, is this: he remembered how it was in his previous life. The joy of being with his Father outweighed all the pleasures of sin.

My father died in 1993. He was a good father. He got better at the father role as he grew older. I miss him.

Imagine this hypothetical, impossible scenario: God comes to me one day and tells me that he is offering me a choice.

Option number one: I can sin all that I want for twenty-four hours. There will be no penalty; none of the sins will count against me in this world or in the life to come. I can choose the most profitable and/or pleasurable sins imaginable.

Option number two: I can have twenty-four hours with my dad again on this earth. Dad will be healthy and in his right mind. I can only choose one of these options.

Which option do you think I would choose?

Anyone with a good father, who has been dead for years, would have no problem making that choice. I would not hesitate in deciding on my daddy. Are you kidding me? One day to be with him, to thank him for his love and for all he did for me? One day to show him his grown grandchildren and what fine young men and women they have become? A day to introduce him to our grandchildren he never met; to hug him once more; to take pictures and videos; to ask him what heaven is like? One day to tell him that the Astros finally made it to the World Series and that his other son, Richard, bought me a World Series ticket? (I might not tell him that they were swept by the White Sox in four straight. Why ruin a perfectly good day for him?)

Jesus had the hope of more than one day with his Father. Jesus had the rest of eternity to be back with the Father! One day for me to have my daddy back would propel me to say no to any sin temptation. What might believing that we have the promise of eternity with our Father do for those temptations and us? If we really believed it, saying no to any temptation might just be possible.

"For the joy set before him he endured the cross" (Hebrews 12:2 NIV). "And now, Father, glorify me in your presence with the glory I had with you before the world began" (John 17:5 NIV).

Those two statements give us insight as to why Jesus said no to sin every time. Somehow, Jesus remembered time with his Father before he came to this earth. His memories were enough for him to know what he was missing and to anticipate the reunion. He endured the cross for the joy to come. It reminds me of Moses, refusing the pleasures of sin for a short time, because "he was looking ahead to his reward" (Hebrews 11:26 NIV). To Jesus, that reward was more real than all the sins that Satan put before him.

A dear friend of mine was one of the best preachers I had heard. Years ago, he "snapped." He began drinking and drugging. He cheated on his wife. He left his family one day, a broken and dazed man. He then returned twenty-two years later.

"Are you ever tempted," I asked him, "to go back to those sins?"

"Yes," he said, "but you know, it is not worth it. Sin pales in comparison to what I have and what I am going to have. It is just not worth it."

Jesus somehow, at some point, remembered his time with the Father. There must be something unbelievably incredible about being with the Father. There is no comparison between the pleasures of sin and the joy of being with the Father. So he said no to Satan. "Daddy," "Abba Father," overwhelms sin and strips it of its power.

To Jesus, sin was just not worth it.

And to Jesus, sin's temptation was not powerful enough. Satan's attacks on Jesus (Matthew 4, Luke 5) failed because, in big part, Jesus knew the Father. He had no doubt that the Father loved him and that the Father would empower him to say no to temptations. Perhaps he remembered the rebellion of the angels in heaven. He certainly, somehow, from reading scripture, from experience, from others, and perhaps from memory was convinced that the Father has no equal. Thus, every time sin reared its head, he knew the Father would deliver him. The Spirit of his Father propelled Jesus to say, "Are you serious?" to each temptation. I can almost hear him say at times, "Really, Satan? Choose you over my dad? There is no comparison." Simply, he trusted the Father to do what the Father had promised. There is no betrayal or broken promises with this Father.

Many of us have had similar experiences with our fathers. "Go ahead and jump," our fathers said as they waited in the pool, and as we, the sons or daughters, contemplated taking the initial plunge. When we finally trusted, and they caught us as promised, bravado grew as we jumped over and over. Because of being human, as life continued, there were times when our dads perhaps dropped us. Sadly, there are those who were never caught by their fathers. Jesus knew without doubt that his Abba, his Daddy, would never drop him.

Also, Jesus understood, better than all of us, the need he had of the Father. "Very truly I tell you, the Son can do nothing by himself; he can do only what he sees his Father doing, because whatever the Father does the Son also does" (John 5:19 NIV). There was not a hint of arrogance in Jesus. He totally relied on his Abba Father.

And get this: every victory over temptation that Jesus experienced was done with the same power that is available to us today. He was a human, a man. "For this reason he had to be made like them, fully human in every way" (Hebrews 2:17 NIV). He does not appear, as tradition states, to be one hundred percent God and one hundred percent human at the same time, while he was on this earth. For instance...

- God cannot be tempted to sin. Jesus was tempted in every way we have or will be tempted.
- God does not need to sleep. The apostles had to awaken Jesus on the boat during the storm.
- God is spirit; Jesus had flesh and blood. When the spear slashed his side on the cross, he bled a lot.
- God never grew physically weary. Jesus, tired as he was from the journey, sat down by a well one day.
- God cannot sin; Jesus became sin.
- And the really big one: God can never die; Jesus cried out in a loud voice, and gave up his spirit.

Jesus indeed "let go" of being equal with God when he journeyed to this earth (Philippians 2:6–7 NIV). He became the person we were meant to be in the beginning.

The keys to victorious living for Jesus and for us are love for and trust in the Father.

We can only love the Father and trust in the Father when we see, feel, experience, and realize his love for us.

God's Suicide

> The reason my Father loves me is that I lay down my life—only to take it up again. No one takes it from me, but I lay it down of my own accord. I have authority to lay it down and authority to take it up again.
>
> John 10:17-18 (NIV)

Please remember Psalms 103 referred to earlier. God remembers how we were formed, that we are but dust. Take note that God, both the Father and the Son, knows that there is a huge difference between him and us. And he realizes it is his *fault*, in the sense that he created us. Along with this, God realizes that if there is any saving to be done, it must be initiated by him and only him, and that we are totally incapable of pulling ourselves up to his level.

Thus Jesus relentlessly plunged on to the abyss of darkness, the cross. He was tempted to skip the final exam and go back home. The "Father, if it be possible" prayer was real. Jesus felt a holy tug that resulted in real temptation to forego the cross and go home: "If there is another way, if there could be another way, please, Father, find it." The tears and the sweat were real. Temptation to forget the agreed-upon plan confronted the only Son of the Father. *Certainly there is a Plan B*, Jesus surmises.

"My soul is overwhelmed with sorrow to the point of death" (Matthew 26:38 NIV).

He spoke those words to men as weak and sinful and faithless as we are or have been. He knew their spinelessness to come. He witnessed their pointless fear when he, the Master of the wind and the waves, and the Creator of all, was in the boat with them. He most certainly knew they would crumble when the pressure mounted. He knew he would have to pinch hit for each of them in the bottom of the ninth with the bases loaded. The only problem was there was no one else left on the bench. It was those guys or no guys.

Yet he pleaded with them to help him at the most critical moment in history. I again say the story is so unbelievable that no one could make it up.

Then why did he appeal to them for help? Because he was human, he was made like his brothers in every way, as the Hebrew writer stated. He was overwhelmed with sorrow. Humans need other humans. Adam needed Eve even with God present. Jesus needed weak, sinful men even with his Father present.

Why was he so sorrowful? He knew that he came for this very moment; he knew he had to die for us to live; he knew the Father's will was for him to go to the cross. He knew all of this, didn't he?

So why the sorrow? Because he was about to go where he had never gone. He was going to go to a place where the Father was not.

How can we humans even come close to *getting* this? "In the beginning was the Word, and the Word was with God, the Word was God" (John 1:1). There was never a time, not one moment, when God was away from... God. God is one. There were times when God went on a mission, away in a sense from himself. Jesus, the Word who became flesh, was not with the Father as he had once been. Philippians 2 says that he let go of being equal with God. But he still had communion with his Father and heard his voice a few times; he was a dutiful Son; he called home daily.

The concept of God I have had for years, along with many others, just doesn't help here. For me, I once thought that God was so together that he was almost emotionless. He knew all the answers, saw things clearly, decisions were easy. I had this concept firmly entrenched because I rarely read the Bible and more rarely gave serious thought to what I accepted as true about God.

Certainly, an honest reading of scripture shatters that concept. Jesus dreaded the cross because he had never experienced a relationship crisis with his Father, and he was smart enough to know that things were going to be different. Darkness was about to engulf him. He was going to feel like a sinner, for he was going to experience all the effects of all our sins.

Since 2007 my wife and I have conducted Grief Recovery Retreats through our foundation, Spark of Life (sparkoflife.org). Those who have experienced devastating loss come to these three-day retreats with broken hearts. Part of the recovery process involves accepting a very painful truth—life can never be the same again after such a terrible loss.

How can it be? If we are waiting for life to return to normal, we will wait a long, long time. Once grievers buy into that, hope can return.

Jesus is the truth. He defines *truth*. Jesus knows reality. The reality is that once Jesus experiences sin, and with it the nails and blood and death, things will never again be the same. The once pure relationship he had with the Father has been shattered. But though it can never be the same again, his relationship with the Father actually will be richer and even more fulfilling. "He always lives to intercede for them" (Hebrews 7:25 NIV). He knows the devastation of sin. He understands more than ever the curse of having a human body marred by sin and death. The Hebrew writer states that even Jesus had to be perfected, as he learned obedience from what he had suffered" (Hebrews 5:5-8 NIV).

Before the cross, Jesus never had any guilty feelings. He never said a word he wished he could take back. He had never disappointed his Father, who was the only Being he sought to please. He knew things were about to change.

Do you remember sinning and realizing it? Your choice hurt someone you loved dearly, and guilt engulfed you? However, none of us have ever experienced the full consequences of our sins. Jesus was on the verge of feeling not only your sin effects, but also that of every human who has ever sinned. That is beyond our ability to fully grasp.

Jesus, though God in the flesh, and God the Father as well, could not possibly know the feelings of separation fully until separation came. "Father, ...take this cup from me" (Luke 22:42 NIV) was expressed though he certainly already knew the answer. There was no other way. The Son knew that. He knew the Father would not ask him to do something that drastic if it were not necessary. Then why pray it? Because the coming darkness overwhelmed him. Jesus, the perfect One, always close to his Father, was about to enter into a realm where his Father's archenemy had gone. It is not a pleasant story; though it is the greatest story.

So Jesus hesitated in the garden about going through with the cross. I am glad hesitation is not a sin. I certainly do not blame him for this momentary reluctance. The brilliant light of the world was about to willingly enter utter darkness. How can one like me, one who has been in darkness and tasted the darkness, totally understand the intense feelings of Jesus as he faced what was truly unknown for him? God the Father, the all-knowing God, was also crashing the *known* barrier and cascading into the dark world of the *unknown*. The Father had never experienced one moment of absolute separation from his only Son.

That Friday, those three hours in particular, was one black, dark Friday afternoon. How could the sun shine as the Son who created the sun died? And how could Holy God look on the Son who had now become sin?

The story is *the* story. There is no other story that rivals it. It is God doing whatever it took to reach us. And whatever it took was his suicide.

There have been many descriptions written about the absolute horrors of crucifixion. Jesus experienced excruciating pain. Those who have researched the details of crucifixion believe, almost without exception, that form of execution is the absolute worst one can imagine. I will not detail it here. I suggest that you look it up for yourself, and see if you do not agree with the experts. The movie *The Passion of the Christ* attempted to capture that horror, and although the movie did it better than anyone else, it fell far short of the true horror. Had Mel Gibson depicted every detail, I doubt if the movie would be lawful to show in public.

The question begs an answer: why this way God? The answer is the answer he gave his Son in the garden when he asked, "Father, is there another way for us to save the world? If so, I beg of you, please find it!"

When the soldiers arrived, as Jesus was begging his Father for the third time, the answer was clear: "There is no other way, Son." The Son, the only Son, the beloved Son—when he saw the arrest party coming, uttered incredible words that help us see his absolute devotion not only to his father, but also to you and me. "Rise! Let us go. Here comes my betrayer" (Mark 14:42 NIV).

My question for God is similar. I liken this to our four-year-old granddaughter's current litany of questions that can be described by one simple word: *why?*

"Why are you sweating, Papa?"

" Because I am hot."

"Why are you hot?"

"Because it is 104 in the shade."

"Why is it 104?"

"Because it is."

"Then why..."

Why, God, is this the only way? If you are all-powerful and can do anything, then could not you devise a less-painful plan?

The answer makes a little more sense if somehow I can see that God will stop at nothing to save us. The reason his response to our sin problem was so extraordinary might be that he feels totally responsible. He brought us into this world; we freely choose to sin; he knows we cannot save ourselves; he devises the plan that will work. The story has no rivals. The worst suffering came to the One who deserved it the least. The innocent Being was slaughtered unmercifully for the guilty. The absolute worst-case scenario happened to the Father and Son—death of their relationship!

God knows life is not fair. "In this world you will have trouble" (John 16:33 NIV), he once shared with his friends mere hours before he was to leave them. He knows how we are formed. He knows we do not "know what we are doing" when we sin. He knows we are born to ultimately die. He knows each of us will one day sin. He knows the story must not only be a good one, but the most compelling one. He knows this world is the only world we know at this time. Thus, a call to come to him and leave this world must be rooted in the greatest love ever shown.

And the cross fills all those requirements.

Only the cross.

Jesus, *refusing* sin and then *becoming* sin, or in other words, his suicide, teaches us two life-changing truths that, if believed, will profoundly change us. One is the incredible power of the Father. The other is intimately connected—our incredible value to him as his children.

PART II
THE HIGH STAKES OF BEING HUMAN

God Is Not Enough?

> In my heart I am an eagle who desires to soar, but also a hippopotamus who loves to wallow in the mud.
>
> —Carl Sandberg

The title appears blasphemous to believers in an all-powerful, all-everything God. All believers, or so it seems, would confidently say that God is indeed enough. However, scripture might disagree. No, let's just say it: scripture, God himself, disagrees. God is the one who states that he is not enough for Adam.

Genesis 2:18, which most of us have heard quoted often, especially in marriage ceremonies, says, "The Lord God said, 'It is not good for the man to be alone. I will make a helper suitable for him.'" So he did.

Previously, I assumed that Adam had it made. He had a beautiful garden, great food, no mosquito bites. He experienced a real closeness to God, walking with him, talking to him. Adam would not have needed a doctor, any meds whatsoever, or life or medical insurance. There would be no trash to take out, bosses to argue with, or ball teams to develop ulcers over. April 15 was just another day in Paradise for him. No disease, body aches, or gray hair. No dentists to fear. No politics to haggle over. This list could go on and on, couldn't it?

But it was not enough. Everything was good in God's creation but one very important item—Adam's aloneness. Even God could not fill the loneliness in Adam simply by his (God's) being. There needed to be another being like Adam.

God was not enough. Better yet, God plus Adam were not enough. If Adam remained alone, all there would be for God to love would be himself and Adam.

God is indeed a "jealous" God who desires that we have no other gods but him (see Exodus 20:5). However, God has no ego problem. He did not pout and feel sorry for himself because Adam felt lonely. There was no "Why do you treat me this way, Adam? Do you not know that I am God and can fill your every need?" No. God, the perfect and loving God, understood the hole in Adam's heart. And in his wisdom, he created woman for Adam so that he might experience a oneness with another being, much as God was experiencing with... God. God the Father had God the Son and God the Spirit with whom to be One. Adam, the human, had…?

Why was Adam lonely? It was because he was created for communion out of the community of the Godhead. The ultimate communion is with our Creator. But God with me only is not true oneness, for it is Creator with creation. For humans to get to true oneness, we *must* have other humans. Our community must be with others in our community. We cannot separate communion and oneness with God from oneness with one another. "That is why a man leaves his father and mother and is united to his wife, and they become one flesh" (Genesis 2:24 NIV). "No one has ever seen God; but if we love one another, God lives in us and his love is made complete in us" (1 John 4:12 NIV).

Often, churches have mission statements displayed in their buildings. I have seen one similar mission statement in many churches that basically state – 'we exist as a church to love God and then to love others.' It might be more appropriate to tweak that statement to read –'We exist as a church to love God *by* loving others.'

God created Adam with his own image *in* Adam. Since God exists in community, and experiences love within that community (oneness), so too must God's likeness have oneness, else it would not be in his image. So Eve was created also in the image of God to create a community in which we will not be alone. Let's repeat what God said a long time ago, "It is not good that man is alone" (Genesis 2:18 NIV).

God breathed into man the breath of life. Life has this strange characteristic: life likes to live. Death is usually unbecoming to life. So humans have an innate desire to live and to procreate themselves to continue living.

God created two avenues for life to be life—marriage and the community of believers he calls the church. The church is to be one, even as the Father and the Son are one. We are to love each other, both in the church and in our marriages, by giving ourselves to each other, thinking of the other above self. When we do that, life becomes real life.

I almost hate to use the terms *church* and *marriage* to describe life because so many have had mostly death experiences in these two arenas. But think about it, the two avenues through which God has given us community are both compared to the unity of the God community. We commune with God as we share community with one another. So of course marriage and the church have been the center of Satan's attacks.

Let me ask you a question I have used with numerous groups. Would you take a gift of $1 billion under this condition: You must live on a deserted island with perfect weather. Your money could build you or buy you absolutely anything you desired—houses, golf courses, gardens, yachts, and the like. You would have the greatest food in the world, everything and anything.

There is only one restriction: no human contact, ever. That means no phone calls to or from friends or family; no Skype; no text messaging or Internet chats; not even old-fashioned mail. You cannot see or talk or communicate in any way to any human being ever again. You cannot even give money to any human being.

Would you take the billion dollars under those conditions?

I know of no one in his or her right mind who would do so. Every one of us would turn down the money; anyone who would dare accept it would be sent to the nearest therapist.

Certainly, we get the point. Humans are vital to this thing we call living. Each of us has a dynamic purpose for being here. God is in effect stating to all of us that we matter, that we are essential, that he *needs* us.

Stating that the uncaused cause needs us confuses me. For the omnipotent One who needs no one outside of himself for him to exist, who is totally complete and whole within himself, for this supreme being to have such a high opinion of human beings excites me. How can God need anything outside of himself, especially if that anything includes me?

In earlier days, especially those graduate school days, I would dare not think such thoughts, much less believe them. For one, I wanted to get that diploma. For another, I had no desire to be labeled a blasphemer of God. And finally, I did not believe such heretical babble. God needing totally sinful, weak David? Who did I think I was? Honestly, writing this I feel as if I just forfeited my Most Humble Award for 1998, which hangs proudly in my office for all to see.

But I also did not buy into the God-loves-David deal. If he does not need me, how can he love me? Oh, I preached it and taught it and counseled many to accept it. But deep in my heart I knew better. God loves the world, but God is disappointed with David. He really does not love me as much as he loves others. After all, as another David said before me, I knew my sins, and they were ever before me. God's needing one who constantly fails in the overcoming-sin game, and thus loving him, appeared to be a contradiction. Anyway, so I thought, he doesn't *need* me. When I feel unneeded, my self-worth falls beneath the safe zone.

So I hereby declare that I am finished with those days. God not only loves me, he delights in me. He adores me. And he needs me. My holy, holy God needs sinful, little-faith, pathetic me! What an honor; what a challenge; what a purely delightful, somewhat scary thought. God really does belong in my boat.

The God of the Unexpected

> When the Lord began to speak through Hosea, the Lord said to him, "Go, marry a promiscuous woman and have children with her, for like an adulterous wife this land is guilty of unfaithfulness to the Lord."
>
> Hosea 1:2 (NIV)

Joseph appeared to be in a real predicament. His fiancée was pregnant, and he knew he was not the father. And then the angel appeared.

When angels appear, they indeed change things. So instead of ending the engagement, he made a wise decision—he married Mary and unofficially adopted the child. We can only imagine the abuse he must have endured.

Then the baby was born, gifts were brought, angels sang, and all was right in his world. And then that angel showed up again.

"Get up and forget going home. Take the child and his mother and escape to Egypt. Stay there until I show up again. Oh, and by the way, the child's life is in danger. Herod will be looking for you. His desire is to kill the baby" (see Matthew 2:13).

And so Joseph did. In the middle of the night he packed up their things and traveled to Egypt.

Now I must admit that I admire this man Joseph, even though we do not know much about him. We know his father was Jacob, his grandpa was Matthan, and his great-grandfather was Eleazar. That's not much.

Still, we know enough. We know he was a man of great honor and integrity. We know he was humble. And we know he listened to angels and did exactly what they said.

What would I do had it been me? I can see me marrying the woman, even though she was carrying a child that was not mine. After all, I had trouble getting a date when I was Joseph's age. Yes, I tell myself, I might have gone ahead with the wedding.

But after the birth and the angels and the wise men, I might have been a bit more aggressive with the deal about going to Egypt. My logic might have gone something like this:

> Pardon me, Gabriel, but may I ask a question here? Why Egypt? That place does not have good vibes with me. Perhaps you remember my ancestors had some problems there. Escape to Egypt? Now that's pretty funny. I would much prefer San Diego or perhaps Austin. I hear the weather is nice, and I already know the language. I have been a fairly receptive, flexible person, don't you think? Not to brag or anything, but do you know many who would have believed this virgin-yet-pregnant story? Let's at least talk about it.

My wife and I are the parents of four children. They are all grown; "out on their own," we like to say. They still call home at times and occasionally share bad news. Some of those times they tell us really bad news. We cry and agonize with them. I simply cannot imagine encouraging them to go to a place where the pain might appear to be worse. And I'll be totally honest, whatever that means. I guess one can be honest and then totally honest is more honest? No, *totally honest* means "this level of honesty might just get me into trouble."

If I am the parent, and my kids are suffering, and I have the power to protect them from more hurt, I doubt if sending them to Egypt would even cross my mind.

PETER AND THE BOATS

I would love to see how Peter's wife decorated his office. Though this of course is pure speculation, I am imagining that the theme centered on boats, such as boats in a bottle, pictures of various boats, and boat coasters. I'm thinking that the biggest picture in his office would be hanging in a spot where Peter would see it everyday. The painting would depict a boat with some of Peter's friends inside it, but with Peter outside the boat in the water, gasping for air and drowning. Jesus is standing on the water, with a hand reaching down, pulling Peter to safety.

And herein lies the entire story of God and us.

God loves us. God knows we are worth everything to him. We are worthy because he created us. We struggle to understand our worth, so we try everything else to "worthify" ourselves: accomplishments, money, power, fame, games, momentary highs from drugs, alcohol, sex, shopping, or possessions. Nothing ever works permanently. Ultimately, sin engulfs us and paralyzes us. We tend to accept mediocrity as our middle names, perhaps our entire names.

We, along with Peter, do not think God and we belong in the same boat. God can row his boat just fine without me, perhaps even better without me. "Get out of my boat!" both Peter and we cry to God. Eventually, we forget he called us out of the fishing-for-fish boat to the fishing-for-people boat, with Jesus in the boat with us. We even try to go back to our safer boat, because we tried and failed the Jesus-in-our-new-boat game. When we tried this evasive maneuver, we found Jesus walking on the shore, making us breakfast. Every time we try to run away from him, he shows up yet again.

"UN-NEEDY" GOD NEEDING US?

Why is Jesus (God) determined to climb into our boats? I asked earlier how could God need anything outside himself. If God is God, and I think that makes sense, then God cannot possibly need anything or anyone outside of himself. Yet scripture appears to teach that God needs us.

There must be an answer to this supposed dilemma. Follow my logic for just a moment. I know this request has danger written all over it (just ask my beloved wife, because my logic seldom wins an argument with her).

God needs nothing outside of himself, either for him to exist or to add to his being. God needs humans (Genesis 2). Therefore, the only logical conclusion is that we humans are not outside of God *and have never been outside of God.*

But sin separates us from our *natural* habitat; thus sin does not and cannot satisfy for long. There is a hole in our hearts, a restlessness that is difficult to explain. We have in one sense always existed, because we all come from the one source, the heart of God. When God created Adam, he formed a body first, then he breathed into that body the breath of life. Thus we have always been in God's breath. Scripture proclaims that God placed eternity in our hearts. We naturally long for something more in our lives, but nothing on this earth really fulfills. C.S. Lewis described this as a kind of "homesickness" for God.

Peter, the one who pleaded for Jesus to get out of his boat, because Peter was a wicked and sinful man, years later startled his readers, then and now, with these words: "We may participate in the divine nature" (2 Peter 1:4 NIV). Jesus, the one who finally convinced Peter that *both* of them belonged in the boat, prayed before he died that we all would understand that ultimate *oneness* is defined as "both God and humans participating together as one." There is another place other than this world, Jesus told his friends (see John 14). We do have eternity in our hearts, because we came from the eternal One.

The story of the incarnation might not be as farfetched as previously thought, though of course it remains farfetched to our human brains. The *Logos* was able to become human and save us because being human is very close to being God. I can feel the skepticism rising as I type these words, and no one is reading this but the one who is writing it!

Most might assume God is capable of becoming anything he desires, even a dog or a cat, but dogs and cats are not made in God's image. Had God become a dog, he could not have even thought about God, much less loved him and obeyed him. If he had become a dog that could think about God, long to obey him, and talk about him, then that would not really be a dog, would it? Dogs cannot do such things.

But God became a human being, made as we are in every way. Jesus could think and talk about God, long to obey him, and long to return from whence he came. How? Do not make the mistake that I have made most my adult life, assuming Jesus was not really as we are. Hebrews 2 proclaims I was wrong in my assumption. Jesus had to be made as we are in every way. The implications are truly life changing. Humans can think and talk about God, *and our yearnings for something more in this life are actually longings to return from where we originated—the heart and breath of God.*

There is no reason for God to become a non-human. There would be no redemptive quality in his becoming a dog. He would just be a dog. No, God became human, in order to save humans. It was a long, long trip from heaven to a fetus, simply not as long as I previously believed.

The incarnation still baffles most of us because we humans are not God. Philippians 2:6–7 validates that, stating that Jesus had to let go of being equal with God. Jesus had to empty himself of certain God-only characteristics to become human. The reason centers on the death issue. God cannot die. Jesus, to save us, had to be made as we are in every way. He had to be tempted as we are, had to overcome sins, had to become sin *for* us, and experience the wages of sin, which is death. Thus, sinless Jesus, now the "sinner" on the cross, had to die the worst possible death.

The pre-incarnate God could not do any of the above necessary requirements to appease his holiness and justice. The enormity of sin he carried demanded the worst death. But because he actually *had* no sin, it was impossible for death to keep its hold on him (see Acts 2). In all this supposed *nonsense* of the story, it actually can begin to make *sense.* "But we preach Christ crucified: a stumbling block to Jews and foolishness to Gentiles, but to those whom God has called, both Jews and Greeks, Christ the power of God and the wisdom of God" (1 Corinthians 1:23, 24 NIV). "And now, Father, glorify me in your presence with the glory I had with you before the world began" (John 17:24 NIV) could be our prayer as well.

The preceding very confusing discourse might appear irrelevant to many. Perhaps it is. For one who has struggled for years to really accept this love and to know the love Paul dubbed "unknowable," these thoughts energize me. They help me to recognize my true self. I am made from the breath of God, destined for his glory, able to participate in the divine nature. We were created from God and naturally have this innate desire to return to God.

We all struggle to discover our reason for being on this earth. Life tends to wear us down. Temptations clamor for our attention and our loyalty. "Give up" lurks around the corner. I need to know I have a reason for being here that makes the pain of living worth it. I am tired of the words mediocrity or apathy emerging everywhere I turn.

Through the years, numerous people have poured out their hearts in my office. Tales of abuse, addictions, sins, failures, and loss dominate the conversations. The one common theme is a kind of identity theft. The couple that has lost a child becomes "the couple whose child died." The drug addict's identity becomes exactly that—"Oh, there goes Joe, the drug addict." The one who cheated on his wife is forever known, or so it appears, as "the adulterer."

In our work with grievers, it is stressed that if my loss becomes my identity, then chances are I will continue in the pit of grief and never get out. At times I will be so sick of the pit that I will try to climb out, only to slide back down, perhaps deeper than before. Breathing that fresh air outside of the pit seems abnormal. It is as if I do not deserve to truly live again. If my identity is tied to my loss ("I am the one whose child died"), then getting out of that pit will seem impossible to me. Ask the woman who experienced five failed marriages, who served water to Jesus one day at a well. In her mind, *that* was her identity—"the woman who failed five times."

Somehow, in some way, I must re-define myself. Actually, it is no redefinition; what I need to know about myself is that I am not defined by my past, failures, sins, hurts, or pains. My true definition is that I am human! And being human equates to being the one God loves and adores. Being human means I was created to participate in the divine nature. Please tell me what God does all day, what he has always done, what he continues to do. I will repeat in case you have forgotten, or if by some weird inexplicable reason you disagree, God has never done anything in his existence that did not concern you and me. Thus, God sat down one day and talked to one we have labeled as the "woman at the well." (See John 4.) Jesus not only received a fresh drink of water himself but also gave living water to a battered soul. For the first time, she saw her true identity!

I need to know this: being human is a blessing and a privilege. It is an honor to be God's child. I did nothing to *earn* this privilege, but I certainly *have* this privilege. And I dare not waste it. Being human is indeed "high stakes." I know this because of Jesus. People I have known validate this realization. You know them too. They are all around. Incredible people, flawed and sinful, being God-like, in spite of their humanness.

GO MARRY AN ADULTERESS

God, it appears, frequently tells people to do things they normally would not even consider doing. "Moses, go and persuade Pharaoh to let his free workforce (hundreds of thousands of people) go free" (see Exodus 3:10). I can imagine my response had I been Moses. And no, I will not share it with you. It would reveal the shallowness of my faith.

"Abraham, take your son, your only son by the way, and kill him. Yes, the son I promised to you in your old age, the son who must live in order for me to be faithful, through whom I told you I would bless the entire world. *That* son, Abraham. And you heard me correctly—kill him, and I do not mean *have* him killed. *You* kill him. And it is a burnt offering. I am sure you know what that means. Now, what are you waiting for? Get up and do it" (see Genesis 22:1–19).

That incident might be the most difficult to explain. The next one however is almost equally perplexing. God picked out a wife for one of his children.

"Hosea, it's about time you got yourself a wife. I have one in mind. And since you are my servant, this isn't exactly a suggestion. And you know me, Hosea, I usually come right to the point. She has the spirit of adultery all over her. She will not be faithful to you. She will break your heart, often. Her sins will negatively influence the three children she will bear you. Your life with her will be a roller coaster of emotions. She is the one for you. Now go court her, marry her, and have children with her" (see Hosea 1:2). And thus the story begins, a story many call the second greatest story in the Bible.

I make no claim to understand totally the God who would command people to do such things. Some scholars apparently cannot reconcile this either. So these stories, they claim, are just that—made up by God to get his point across. When discussing the Hosea dilemma, one person I know said he knows it is just a story, for no one would name his child Gomer in real life.

But for all the things about God that I do not quite grasp, here is one I do get: trying to predict what God might do, or how he works, is useless. When God does or asks the unthinkable, we might as well examine that and seek to understand, for if God exists, there must be moments of total misunderstanding and confusion.

This we can grasp: when God tells any human to do something, he must believe that the human can do it. God's opinion of his children is much like our opinion of our children, except infinitely higher. He knows that for which we were created. *It was his breath (life) that he breathed into us.*

So God does tell stories and uses real-life drama with real people being asked to do incredible things to help us *get* him. When we do, the sun comes out from behind the clouds, and God makes more sense even in the midst of our confusion.

Forgiveness

> Jesus said, "Father, forgive these people! They don't know what they're doing."
>
> Luke 19:34-35
> (Contemporary English Version)

All the evidence, from our being here to the cross, shouts that God loves each of us, even as much as he loved Jesus. Along with the majority of Christians I know, I have struggled with accepting that love fully. I suppose there are many reasons. For one, I know how sinful I am. I once sat down and began writing all my sins that I could remember. I think I made it to the third page of the legal pad when this feeling of disgust washed over me. How could God love me as much as he loves others? And how could he really ever forgive me? The whole concept of forgiveness confuses me.

We know so much about forgiveness. We know we cannot live one day without it. We are usually lousy at dispensing it. Some people are simply easy to forgive (they are usually the ones who love us, think we are wonderful, shed tears begging us to forgive them, and come with a box of chocolates). We know forgiveness when it happens, from others to us or from us to others. We know when we fake it and when others fake it. We know we like it, a lot. And this I know: forgiveness is God's middle name.

I know nothing about forgiveness. I am clueless why God continues to forgive me, and for that matter, why he forgave me in the first place. I do not have any ability or desire to forgive certain people or how to begin the process of forgiving at times. Forgiving is absolutely the most difficult command I find in scripture, along with five or ten others that I, at times, think are also the most difficult. At the very best, forgiveness confuses me; at the worst, it *really* confuses me. I do not know how God discovered it or why he created it. And if he did create it, then why does he need to discover it, in me at least.

Certainly, the above two wordy paragraphs are an exaggeration. For if I know *anything* at all about forgiveness, then I do not know *nothing* about it. (Now I am confused. But that sentence, I think, is good English. If it isn't, then it is what it is. See Yogi Berra for clarification.)

So there you have it. Forgiveness is confusing. But God says it is essential, that we receive it and accept it, and that we give it to others. And not just to *some* others, but to *all* others.

I want to receive it, I need to accept it, but I fight against giving it. And the big question is why?

My wife and I through the years have helped lead marriage retreats at various places around the country. One particular retreat stands out in my mind. Twenty couples gathered together for a few days to find out if their marriages could be saved. On the first morning, as the couples arrived and found nametags and coffee, the mood was, shall I say, just a bit somber. My wife and I went about the room greeting people with a smile and a handshake. We did not receive many smiles back.

Of the twenty couples, one, by self-admission, had an okay marriage. They were there to turn it around, as they told me. The others were in various places on the happy-marriage scale of 0-20

(0 being the marriage from hell, 20 being the marriage made in heaven). Let's summarize their scores this way: 19 of them were below a 1.

One woman, married for over twenty years and the mother of three, had recently revealed to her husband that she had carried on an affair for many years.

I'll call this couple Joe and Mary. He was a leader in their church, by all accounts a humble, genuine man who truly loved God and others. While in high school, he had withstood sexual temptations to keep himself pure for the wife he had yet to meet. He was a virgin on their wedding night and had been faithful to Mary ever since. Joe provided extremely well for his family, was a great dad, was a leader in the youth group, helped Mary with the dishes, never yelled at the refs at his kids' games, took out the garbage without being reminded, and I am sure picked up his underwear. He was the kind of guy we want our daughters to marry—a really good guy with no skeletons in his closet. Mary agreed with all the above.

Mary felt terrible about the affair. She wore guilt and shame as a filthy garment. She deeply desired for Joe to forgive her and to rekindle the love she still felt for her husband. The affair was over. All the right steps had been taken. Joe knew this was true as well. But she could not answer the obvious why question.

Throughout the retreat, Mary rarely lifted her head and never smiled. She was as defeated and hopeless as anyone we had ever seen. Looking at her, images of the adulterous woman slung at the feet of Jesus in John 8 came to mind. She was guilty as charged, thinking she deserved to be stoned to death. "Let Joe cast the first stone," she seemed to say for three days.

As the last session was wrapping up, I watched as couple after couple re-committed to one another. When their turn came, all Mary could utter were words we had heard often that weekend: "I am so sorry, Joe. Please forgive me and give our marriage one more chance. But I do not blame you if you cannot forgive me. I do not deserve forgiveness."

Joe was as gracious as possible, but understandably a bit cold in his response. "I want to forgive you," he stammered, holding back the tears. "I just do not know how," and who could condemn him or do any better than that?

The retreat ended Saturday night. Eighteen of the couples re-affirmed their love for each other and determined to continue working on their marriages. Joe and Mary were one of those. As they walked out of that room that night, the odds of their making it were slim though.

Two months passed. One day Joe called. He and Mary wanted to come see me. They lived about 500 miles away, so we scheduled one of those all-day marathon sessions. Come in at eight o'clock and leave whenever.

I was apprehensive about the coming meeting. "We trust you," he told me. "We are at a crossroad. We'll decide after our time with you whether we will keep trying or give up."

Thanks a lot Joe, I thought. *No pressure! Just the seventh game of the World Series, bases loaded, two outs, bottom of the ninth, my team trailing by three runs, I step up to the plate... and Sandy Koufax is pitching.*

The day of the meeting, I had asked my wife and a few others to be praying. I had no outline or agenda or any strategy for our time together. Secretly, I was praying for a reprieve from the governor; but alas the phone never rang.

Just as planned, they walked into my office at eight o'clock. For four hours we talked, cried, searched, explored their past, and prayed. Mary was still remorseful, trying to accept God's forgiveness and desperate to receive Joe's. I still had no idea what color her eyes were.

Joe kept stating that he had forgiven her, but no one in the room that day or in heaven for that matter believed him. Finally, around noon, Joe really became honest.

"Look," he began, staring at Mary, "I decided when I became a Christian that I would be a virgin when I married. I prayed for you before I met you. I kept myself pure so my wife would be the only one. I was determined to have a great marriage, one that would honor God. In the twenty-five years we have been married, not once did I break the vows we shared with one another, and I had many opportunities. But I said no to each of them, because I love my wife and my God. I cherished you, provided for you, loved you, and helped with the housework and the kids. I have been a genuine Christian man and been a leader in our church. I am not addicted to pornography, alcohol, golf, drugs, hunting, or anything else. I just do not understand how you could do this. And not just once or twice, but for years? I do forgive you, but..."

After listening to his credentials, I was impressed. Now I wanted my granddaughters to marry a guy like him.

Her response? Not surprisingly, simply more guilt and shame and hopelessness. A nod of agreement, not a word, and her head hung a little lower.

So there we sat. Joe crying, Mary slumping, and I not knowing what to say or to do. Koufax had thrown me a curve; I swung and missed. Strike one.

The day before had been a Sunday. On Sunday nights, our church has almost a thousand college students attend a late communion service. The night before Joe and Mary met with me, I was the speaker. As I walked up to the podium to speak, I did what I rarely do. I ditched my notes and simply shot from the hip, as we like to say. Something within me said to speak on the story of the prodigal son in Luke 15. So I did. I remember saying that this story is about two sons—one who messed up and strayed, and one who was good and stayed. But the heart of the story is the father, who loved both sons.

So on Monday, as we all sat in silence, it hit me suddenly, and I said, "I think God wants us to talk about the prodigal son."

As soon as those words tumbled out of my mouth, Joe and Mary, as one, both looked up, startled. I asked them to explain their sudden interest.

Joe explained, "We stayed at the Hampton Inn last night. When I got up this morning, as we were drinking coffee, I opened the Bible to Luke 15. So I read out loud the story of the prodigal son. I cannot believe you mentioned that story. I guess God wants us to talk about it." Mary nodded enthusiastically in agreement. They both looked at me, as if I had something brilliant to say. Honestly, at that moment, I began to choke. Koufax threw a changeup, and I swung and missed. Strike two.

So for a second or two, silence. Then I decided that if I began to talk, certainly something would come out. And as we like to say, God at times is really cool about his timing.

"It's obvious, isn't it? Mary, in the story you are, without doubt, the son who left. Broken and dazed by the choices you have made, you have crawled back to the Father and begged for forgiveness, but not really expecting a place back in the house. And Joe, you are the good son who stayed home. It is beyond you to throw a party for the stray who has fallen. You have kept all the rules and have been an exemplary son. Your Dad never threw a party for you. You almost resent the easiness of the grace shown, and the forgiveness lavished on your brother.

"But both of you are wrong. Both of you have missed the love of the Father. Joe, you think you deserve a place in the Father's house because you have been so good all these years. And Mary, you do not think you have a place in the Father's house because you have been so bad. Both of you are so wrong. You both are loved by the Father because of *him*. He loves you because you *are*. You both have a place in your Daddy's house."

They both understood. They grasped hands. Joe said it all. He looked at his bride and said with conviction, "Mary, could you find it in your heart to forgive me? I have been so blind, so arrogant. And I do truly forgive you."

She said she had nothing to forgive, but that of course she forgave him.

At that moment, they got up from the couch, looked at me, hugged me, and then Joe said, "Mary, I think it's time we go home, together." And so they did.

Koufax had thrown his best pitch—a fast ball on the outside corner. I closed my eyes and accidentally hit the ball, and a gust of wind blew it over the fence for the game-winning grand slam. Certainly, nothing of my doing.

Now I know two things: one, forgiveness might just be God's first name. And two, Mary's eyes are blue.

A few years after Joe and Mary's reconciliation, I received the following article Joe had written. He gave me permission to use it here.

FINDING FORGIVENESS IN OUR OWN HUMANITY

> While we exert ourselves to grow beyond our humanity, to leave the human behind us, God becomes human; and we must recognize that God wills that we be human, real human beings. While we distinguish between pious and godless, good and evil, noble and base, God loves real people without distinction.
>
> Dietrich Bonhoeffer in *A Year with Dietrich Bonhoeffer: Daily Meditations from His Letters, Writings, and Sermons*

Just a few nights ago, I awoke with vivid recollections of a dream that I had just experienced. Like most dreams that I remember, it was a fusion of the things of reality as well as the things of fantasy. In this dream, I was boarding an airplane and I had become separated from my wife of thirty-three years. I was going through the plane frantically searching for my wife, under seats, in the aisle, in the baggage compartment overhead. Familiar faces kept popping up in my dream of relatives and friends, but nobody on the plane seemed to know where I could find her, and even worse, no one seemed to really care. The search was mine and mine alone to complete. The ambivalence of the attitudes of the bystanders was very distressful, and as my search through the plane continued the frustration grew.

But then suddenly, lying down between two seats in the front of the airplane was my wife. It seemed totally natural that she would be there, nestled among some luggage. I knelt down and put my hand under her neck and brushed away her hair so as to see her face. She turned her head and looked at me, and I spoke to her saying, "Come sit beside me." She then replied, "Ok".

This simple but profound dream marked yet another turning point in my life, which accounts for why when I did wake up, and despite the fact that it was two o'clock in the morning, I wept deeply and praised God for his goodness and thanked Him for His mercy. For years I had dreams of chasing after my wife but not finding her. The framework of the dream was always the same. I was either looking for my wife and could not find her, or she was within my grasp and yet continued to evade me.

In the dreams previous to the other night, no matter how hard I tried to catch up to her, either running or in a car or flying over a mountain–whatever the context of the dream, the essential component of the dream was my inability to find my wife and take hold of her. I cannot say how many times over the last many years that I have awakened to a tightened chest and muscle fatigue, and frequently sadness and tears, as a consequence of those dreams borne of our relationship issues.

The truth is that I have always deeply loved my wife since we were married not long after high school, but after twenty-five years of marriage and three children, she decided that she did not love me. My dreams were telling me this long before I found it out in reality. When I say that I have always loved her, I always have; but how deep that love was to become and to what foundation it would find its anchoring came in a form of life experience that no marriage should ever have to endure. Tragically, the place that she looked for a different experience was built on a fabricated lie–the allure of infidelity. Over a period of a couple of years, as my life slipped more and more into a routine of work commitment and our relationship started to clearly falter, her life slipped over the edge. Instead of following my wife into this abyss, early on, I stood my ground and watched it happen. I was either too proud or too oblivious to the reality of her crisis to intervene. I knew my wife had a problem but I wasn't going to make it mine.

As I watched her move farther and farther away from me, I remember vividly not really knowing what to do about it. She was depressed and distant. I wasn't getting what I needed out of the marriage and I let her know about it. It was only after I opened a note that she had written to a co-worker strewn among some of our tax documents that my proud world crashed in around me in an instant. A huge chunk of my life as I believed it existed was instantaneously changed. I had been betrayed for years. It reduced me to nothing.

The revelation of that fact now five years ago, and how it came upon me like a tornado, has taken me to a place of deeper understanding of the nature of Christ, the nature of sin and our own desperate humanity of choice between them. As I share with you about this journey, I am not painting a rosy picture of this reality. It is not a fairy tale where all is forgotten and we moved on with our happy lives. We live every day with the horror of these choices. I struggle daily with what I know is the vital role of forgiveness giving and forgiveness asking.

I only began to find these truths at the bottom of my life, in a place where I was so desperate for healing of my marriage that my sole resort was to cry out to the Father. I had no other moves. When faced with the awful and dreadful reality of losing not just my wife, but my family, I desperately needed a sliver of hope to hang on to. That hope came in the form of a man named David, who through his own experience, understood and articulated my pain, discussed my unknowns and fears, and told me that our God was indeed faithful and would never abandon us in our time of greatest need. Those words cut through me like a knife. I reached and took hold of that promise. David is a champion.

I don't succumb to the belief that I caused my wife's infidelity, as those choices were singularly hers, and she bears that responsibility alone. Not long after finding out about her affair, I falsely bore some of this guilt in the search for understanding why? The truth is that she made the choice of adultery.

I did not. I cannot deny, however, my own actions and influence in how she came to a place in her life where she would consider making such a terrible choice. It was a decision of reckless abandonment of her responsibilities as my wife, and a betrayal of her responsibilities to her God and her own dignity. I know now, looking back on that period, that I could have done more to help her or to strengthen her, and even perhaps to prevent this from happening, if only I had been a husband who was more like Christ.

As this plague crept upon our lives, I truly believe that I dismissed a lot of her emotional state under the conviction that my wife was weak. As her dependency upon medications increased, so did my disdain. Instead of reaching down into the ditch to give her my hand to hold on to, I seemed complacent in standing on the side of the ditch, looking down, and telling her its depth. I expected her to climb out on her own.

Until God led me to a place where I could clearly see my own sinful nature in similar horror, it was impossible for me to consider any grant of forgiveness for hers. After I had fallen into my own deep ditch I finally recognized the value of a caring extended hand. I was the proud prodigal son, plenty of the facts on my side but little compassion. I was strong but not courageous.

I looked everywhere for another road for salvation, but it became more and more clear that no matter what the outcome of our marriage–healing would only come with forgiveness, which could only be revealed in light of our shared, imperfect humanity. When I was likewise utterly broken, I suddenly knew then the revelation of the kind of love that I had been unwilling to give. It was love without condition.

Instead of throwing in the towel, my wife determined to bear this heart-wrenching agony to reclaim her first love–Jesus. In time, He reconstructed us both anew, and we slowly but purposefully found each other again. We were as broken as two people can be, so if you think it can't be done; you are just wrong. The restoration of our marriage was brought about through our complete desperation.

God placed some of the most beautiful people into our lives at just the times when we needed them the most. Their experience of loss and renewal buoyed our own hopelessness, and their gentle guidance was a light out of our darkness. I cannot deeply express the substance of this miracle. God sent people from everywhere to help us.

It is perhaps unfair to categorize the whole of a life through the criteria of a single event, but most of us can relate to those unique, and often, extremely difficult times in our lives where we faced the crossroad of who we were to become and how we would get there.

I started this essay with the Bonhoeffer quote because in my own experience tragedy is so often the forerunner of understanding: about what it means to live in my real, factual and fragile humanity. When I ultimately moved beyond the fear and anger of her infidelity, came face to face with the reality of losing my wife and seeing the web of my family torn into, all of my manly bravado and pride soon abandoned me.

The experience wrecked me. It stripped away a lot of what I believed was true and what I believed was a foundation in my life. The "man" inside of me wanted retaliation against the predator. I still struggle with this today and cannot say that I am over it. But mostly I lived in a fog for a long time after becoming aware of, and accepting, the reality of her affair.

Were it not for those loving souls that guided me, e-mailed me with encouragement, bombarded me with the promises of scripture, I may have wandered into my own wilderness. My gratitude to those people cannot be overstated. As my friend David told me, "the most beautiful people to God are the most broken ones." That is the kind of love that I now know, and try to give.

Over these intervening years, both my wife and I have had many occasions to speak to other couples about overcoming infidelity and finding a deeper, more lasting love together. How I wish that in my own life journey I had learned these lessons without having to endure the pain associated with the unveiling revelations of their experience. I know that a better example of how to be the right kind of husband, and she the right kind of wife, were right there before us; but we failed to embrace them into acts of daily devotion toward one another.

I justified my love commitment to her through long hours of work and through providing a good lifestyle to our family. She justified her commitment to me through the rearing of our three children in my absence due to extended travel demands of my work. Neither of these beliefs was deep enough in their motivation or commitment to bind the two of us into "one flesh". We started off that way but somewhere over the years, we drifted. Our marriage became more of a business relationship, an exchange arrangement, rather than a mutual dependency.

We operated this way for years, and in my case, oblivious to any vulnerabilities or issues. I had become so emotionally unattached from my wife's needs, that I failed to see the numerous examples that preceded her infidelity, and the signs of where she was being actively stalked by a predator co-worker. I never added up the odd circumstances of her being late from work, or out with her girl friends too many nights without explanation or reason. I too quickly excused the rising influence of her co-worker friends that did not share our historic values.

I offered up more anger than concern over her emotional distancing. Only she can speak to what drove her to take the course that she did, but she has said to many that we have talked with that she first fell out of love with God, then me. The exact circumstances that move someone into an affair are numerous and complicated, but the outcome is always the same. Honest people become liars. Trustworthy people become deceivers. Innocent victims are scattered.

I cannot summon the words to adequately describe this scourge. It kills everything around you, and wrecks not only your own life and that of your partner, but the lives of your children, your parents, your friends, and anyone who loves and cares for you. It has become, I believe, the single most effective tool that Satan uses today to war against not just marriages, but against families. It is glorified on television and in the movies.

Our media is filled with not only its acceptance but its promotion.

Infidelity leads only to grief. Work exhaustively, if needed, on the marriage that you have before you look for happiness in another direction. Affairs are not based in reality. Infidelity can be overcome and the stain can be washed away–but the stench of it remains. There is not a day that goes by that I am not reminded of our experience. The truth now, as I write these words, still remains so difficult to imagine that this actually happened to us, and how great is our regret.

The road that I have taken with respect to being a victim of infidelity, a path of reconciliation and restoration with my spouse, may not be the road for you, but I pray that it will be. Each person makes that choice independently. It is not an easy choice to make. What I would encourage you to act upon is based upon the same profound counsel that I was given by a fellow sojourner, who likewise many years ago found himself in a similar situation.

Particularly as men, we desire to fix these problems quickly and with certainty. We demand quick restitution and total repentance in exchange for our forgiveness and continued support. It's all very conditional. Every bone in my body at the time that I found out about my wife's affair cried out, demanded, more control. But the only way back was to give up those things that had put us there in the first place.

The rebuilding from the necessary unlearning was a small step at a time for us both. I had to be willing to suffer through the time. As badly as I wanted the pain of it all just to end, I determined to bear it. This was the greatest gift that I gave our journey back together; a willingness to suffer through the time.

For much of my adult life, I lived my life in a reverse hierarchy of values, caring more about the idea of things than I did the engagement of them into the human experience. Dealing with concepts was so much cleaner, and I could mold my own reality.

I believe this explains why I was so clueless as to my wife's obvious misery, because I was more in love with the thought of my wife than I was the real, imperfect person. It is messy getting involved with real people. I gave up a lot of myself to heal our marriage, and so did my wife. It was costly because shared humanity is hard.

It requires things of you and sometimes doesn't respond in ways that you desire or imagine. It is much easier to pray for the poor than it is to take a blanket to a homeless individual on a cold winter night. It is much easier to pontificate about the sanctity of life than it is to adopt a child or open your home to an orphan. In the world of real humanity, your goodness is not frequently recognized or rewarded overtly.

Really helping a single person is many times more difficult than imagining helping hundreds. Our culture is pervasively concept oriented and I was a child of our culture. I lived in a world that looked real, but one that I constructed from my own models. The clarity to understand this, and change, was one of the greatest outcomes of our shared suffering.

Through the recognition of my own less-than-perfect existence, it was easier to find compassion in the failings of others. I thought a lot about how God really looks at me and what He sees when he does. To him, my sins were as gut-wrenching as were my wife's. A lot of my pain was tied up in my pride of ownership, not my shared humanity with her.

Through this trying time, Christ's abiding love for me never faltered. His forgiveness of me, without demand, was without hesitation. The healing of our marriage literally took years, not months; but I ultimately found the place in my soul to forgive her and to ask her to forgive me. In doing so, I learned more about my own desperate humanity than I can express.

I came to know how hopeless I am without Christ. Sadly, it took breaking us both into pieces to put us back together right again. My wife emerged from this awful place in her own life to become a champion for Christ. In her weakness and shame, I have witnessed God rebuilding her, through His grace, into a totally new person. He has walked with her from the first instance where she threw herself on the ground in shame, to giving her testimony of hope before hundreds of people.

What I know now, and I've always really known, is that she has always been a better person than I; even in the midst of all of this. Sin has no discrimination in the victims it chooses. Now, the Father is her first love, again.

As a young Christian, I had hoped that my relationship with Jesus would be one filled with happiness, and that He would protect me from the sins of the world. In a twist of irony, I was never unfaithful to my wife and I have never had another sex partner; prior to or since our marriage. Even our marriage counselor said that he could not remember meeting anyone with that unique history relative to today's experience.

My pride in my own fidelity did not protect me from the evils of this world, nor did it excuse my numerous failings as a husband. We have no claim to any special gifts or knowledge beyond that of our own experience, and we only share our painful experience in hope of another's healing. It is not an easy thing to do, to disclose our own personal failings.

As we have totally failed each other in marriage, we have also been totally restored in marriage–through Christ, and He alone. All marriages are framed by the two people in them as a collective, not as two separated. God's unconditional love has taken our relationship to a depth of understanding and mutual commitment that would have been incomprehensible to either of us before our suffering. This is my testimony. We have experienced finding forgiveness in our own humanity, and it is available to us all[14].

The Twenty-First Century Adulterous Woman

> But Jesus bent down and started to write on the ground with his finger. When they kept on questioning him, he straightened up and said to them, "Let any one of you who is without sin be the first to throw a stone at her."
>
> John 8:6-7 (NIV)

The rumor was one of those must-be-true ones. Laura, almost fifty, reportedly was having an affair with someone half her age. I could hardly believe it, but in my heart I finally acknowledged it was probably true. She had been desperately seeking something, anything to make her life bearable. She certainly was not finding it in her marriage.

Laura was a Christian, and apparently serious about her relationship with God. Hypocrisy was an unfit garment for her. I had not seen her or heard from her in a couple of months when I heard the confirmation of the gossip. She had left her husband, her four children, and her just-born twin grandsons. I assumed she left with the young man everyone in her church talked about.

One of her daughters confirmed this to me: her mother had left the country to get as far away as possible.

I have not seen or heard from Laura in years. I heard recently she was living in Europe. Yet she still impacts my life today. I think of her as the twenty-first century adulterous woman.

The original adulterous woman emerged in scripture in John's account of the life of Jesus (John 8). It is a curious inclusion in John's book. Many scholars believe others added this story years later, and it was not part of the original writing of John. Early manuscripts of John omit the story altogether.

I feel a bit ashamed to admit that I have spent hours studying this issue, attempting to determine the authenticity of the story. There is obviously nothing inherently wrong with this kind of study, yet looking back I now question my motives. However, today I believe I have the answer to (1) why I thought it was necessary to validate the account, and (2) why the story absolutely must be true.

First, in those days, I was in graduate school. It was some kind of a kick when someone asked me what I did. "I am in pursuit of my Masters in Theology," I would proudly say, as humbly as I could. *Theology* sounded a great deal more important than *Bible*. It almost made me an instant spiritual person.

"Oh," many would respond, "Then who do you think Cain married, and was creation in real twenty-four-hour days, and who recorded the death of Moses?"

Everywhere I went it appeared people were indeed impressed by my *almost* credentials. Then they would laugh behind my back. I am assuming that to be true, because, to be honest, I was laughing behind my own back, which probably explains my chronic back pain.

For those not in pursuit of their Master's in Theology, I must explain. You see, at the master's level, it is crucial to be able to discuss with some credibility questions that appear to have little to do with real life. I calculated once that I spent at least fifty hours researching whether Isaiah wrote the entire book, which bears his name, and what was up with Proto-Isaiah, Deutero-Isaiah, and Trito-Isaiah, whoever or whatever they were or are.

So I was pre-destined, or at least graduate-school destined, to dissect John 8 and determine its place in the canon. And by the way, what *did* Jesus write on the ground? We never have solved that one.

Second, and much more relevant, my quest to be smart was a classic avoidance maneuver. John 8 and the adulterous woman made me uncomfortable. Sin being revealed for all to see is frightening, especially if my sin is the issue. I simply had no desire to get to the meaning of John 8. If getting to Jesus requires revealing how sinful I am, forget it, especially in the sexual realm. Those who are called "reverend" had better never admit to any sexual struggle, much less to actually have those struggles. That supposed pathway to freedom was simply too heavy a price to pay.

The answer to the question about the validity of the story in John 8 is now quite clear to me. I still do not know exactly where it belongs in scripture, but belong it does.

The story almost screams that it is true. Most certainly it happened. The answer, for me, has little to do with all the study and research of the manuscripts and sources, though of course this might be helpful. The answer is simple: no one could make this up. Jesus, the Jewish teacher, living during that time, would never (so it seems) throw out years and years of tradition and teaching by loving and accepting such a sinful woman. If that story were made up to somehow trick us into believing the deity of Jesus at that time in history, then the fraud would have backfired. The only way the story would have been written was if it actually happened.

Laura's church had evidently concluded that John 8 and the story of the adulterous woman was not part of the original writings, for they acted as if they had never heard of the story, or if they had, did not believe it. Laura was not only condemned, she also was stripped, beaten, and left to slowly bleed to death. Her husband? He was almost canonized.

THE REST OF THE STORY

I found it easy to love Laura and not to condemn her. Why? I knew her story, and I also knew her husband. John was a successful business owner, employing almost a thousand people. He was one smooth operator, so smooth that I had learned not to trust him. For years, I had discovered that John, also a leader in his church, was one great liar. Few, besides my wife, would have believed it. My wife knew it, because she had concluded the same thing about John years ahead of me. She kept warning me about John, that I should be careful and not trust him. When I would ask how she knew this, she would respond, "I just know it. Trust me on this one." I would respond that perhaps there needs to be a bit more empirical evidence and that she might consider enrolling in graduate school, like her esteemed husband.

I apologized later when John went behind my back, lied about me, and cut me out of a business deal. Two people, and two people only, knew the truth. My sweet wife never said those dreaded words, "I told you so," because she knew she had told me so, I knew she had told me so, even our dog knew she had told me so. Anyway, that's what she told me.

Now John was and still is, I suppose, a person of great worth to God. But John was a really bad husband. His wife was slowly dying inside. Years earlier, when they had been married less than a year, Laura caught her husband in an affair. The evidence was irrefutable. When confronted with the sin, John finally admitted it, promising never to do that again and begging her never to tell anyone. She worked on forgiving him and really had. But the sin kept returning, and the pattern continued.

Laura's convictions told her not to give up on her marriage. Though of course not perfect herself, she honestly tried, but John never changed. His unfaithfulness continued. After years of a dead marriage, Laura went to counseling and desperately tried to convince him to go. But he refused. He was too busy keeping up the appearance that they had a great marriage, and that he was a great Christian.

So one day the pain overwhelmed Laura. And she left her husband, her church, her friends, and even her children and grandchildren.

Years later, I was teaching a class in another part of the country. I shared with them Laura's story, initially telling them how Laura had left her husband, her four children, and recently born grandchildren. Then I asked, "What do you think of Laura and John?"

The answers came quickly. Laura, many said (all men), was selfish. She had abandoned not only her husband but also her children. "She had fallen away from God," one surmised. "Probably never *really* loved God," spouted another. "She must be on drugs," one countered. "She is disgusting," another concluded. "Perhaps a lesbian," one whispered, with a flurry of nodding heads.

After Laura's assassination, there was a pause. A hand went up in the back of the room. It was a woman's hand, hesitatingly raised. I knew her quite well. Her marriage was also in shambles. Not many knew, not even her husband. Her story had Laura written all over it.

Her words quieted the lynch-mob mentality that was brewing in the church building that had been built to honor the Christ who was once lynched himself.

"She must have had immense hurt and pain to have left her family."

Hearing these words quieted the class. Shame and guilt seemed to enter the room and take their rightful place. I then told the class the rest of the story. Slowly, more and more began understanding. Sides began shifting from lynching her to actually loving her.

I once had a professor in graduate school who said something profound one day: "Everyone acts the way they do for a reason." Even graduate school can be helpful at times.

Jesus understood that principle. He must have learned it from his Father. When he gazed at the sinful woman in John 8, there was not even a hint of disgust in him. The Son, the only Son, of the Holy, Holy, Holy, God, tenderly looked at one who moments before had been sharing a bed with someone not her husband, with the stench of sin upon her, and Jesus... loved her... and did not condemn her.

How? Why? What is so different about him, and us? The answer is so profoundly simple: Jesus understood her story.

"Father, forgive her," he seems to say. "For she does not know what she is doing."

So to Laura, wherever you are: may you find yourself slung to the feet of the Holy Jesus. And may you hear his words that he spoke to the original adulterous woman and to you. May you see the Father who knows all your sins but loves you anyway, for he knows your story.

And to John: may you, too, see Jesus. He loves you as much as he loves Laura. He knows your story as well.

And to the rest of us: perhaps it is time to drop our stones. Everyone has a story.

Hope Hopes

> And hope does not disappoint, because the love of God has been poured out in our hearts through the Holy Spirit who was given to us.
>
> Romans 5:5 (NIV)

It was a beautiful fall day. I was in my office studying when someone knocked on the door. It irritated me a bit, because I had no appointments that day. Usually when those with no appointments come wanting to talk with me, they went through my secretary, and she would buzz me. So I reasoned that it was simply some well-meaning church member who would come into the office and ask the one question most preachers get many times a day: "Preacher, are you busy?"

But I answered the door against my better judgment, and I'm so glad I did. Behind that door stood a distraught, beautiful, twenty-year-old. Her name was Hope. But her looks defied her name. She obviously had been crying for a really long time.

"May I help you?"

"Yes," she said. "I have to talk to you. It is a matter of life and death. I know I don't have an appointment, but may I please talk to you?"

I invited her in. She told me her story. She had tuned her back on God, had lived with her boyfriend against her parents' will. Her parents had disowned her. She and her boyfriend had been heavy into the drug scene. A month earlier, she found out she was pregnant and foolishly thought he would be excited. When he had demanded an abortion, she refused. So he left her and had been gone for weeks. She had no money, had been kicked out of their run-down apartment, and was reconsidering the life option, not only for her baby, but also for her. Suicide was lurking around the corner. "Give up" was written all over her once-beautiful face.

"I have no hope," she cried. "Isn't that ironic? Here my name is Hope, and I do not know if hope will ever again be real."

Now, please do not judge me too harshly here, but I asked a really dumb question. Believe me, it is a lot easier to come up with an appropriate response now. Then I had one of those "Please, God, *help!*" moments. But God showed up a sentence or two late.

"So why did you come here to this church to see me? I don't think we've met."

"This is the only church I have been in for a long time. I was here for a friend's wedding a couple of years ago."

The really bad question at least gave me a minute to figure out what to say or do next. I grabbed my Bible that was sitting on the desk next to me. I started flipping through it, and suddenly the Bible opened up to John 8 (really). "Do you mind if I read a few verses of the Bible?"

She said she didn't mind, that she had come to a church for help and was kind of hoping for some spiritual guidance. So I began to read the familiar story of the woman caught in adultery, slung at the feet of Jesus by the self-serving, self-righteous religious leaders.

"'Neither do I condemn you,'" I read. "'Now get up, and do not continue to live like this. You were created for something far better than the way you have been living. You can do it.'"

Her response is forever in this brain of mine: "Are you serious? That story is in the Bible? I never have heard it."

She thanked me as her countenance returned with vigor. Her tears went through a discernible transformation, from tears of shame to tears of hope.

And I realized her parents had aptly named her.

Paul, Me, and a Friday Night

> Now the tax collectors and sinners were all gathering around to hear Jesus. But the Pharisees and the teachers of the law muttered, "This man welcomes sinners and eats with them."
>
> Luke 15:1-2 (NIV)

It was half past six when I met Paul at Celebrate Recovery, a Christian twelve-step group. He had been charged with abusing his stepdaughters and was awaiting trial in two weeks. A friend had asked me to welcome him.

I was apprehensive about this assignment. One of our children had been abused years earlier, and thoughts of greeting a child molester rattled me. As I battled anger and guilt over this abuse, Celebrate Recovery became the vehicle for my healing. Me, forgiving the abuser, was not optional. Scripture clearly teaches the absolute necessity of us forgiving others who have sinned against us. And though the odds of forgiving myself were better than forgiving him, I still considered that a long shot. Fathers –

good fathers – do not let their children be abused. My child was abused – under my watch. I was not a 'good' father.

The toughest to forgive was God, who could have and should have, in my way of thinking, stopped it.

So, shaking hands with and 'welcoming' a possible child molester did not exactly thrill me. But there he was, a seventy-year-old man, and there I was. I did not want to shake his hand, and very definitely had no desire to welcome him. So I lied when I told my friend that I would welcome this man. I had decided that later in our groups when we are encouraged to be honest, I could say something like: *"Hello, my name is David, and I struggle with lying, very recent lying. I lied tonight, intentionally lied. I am not sorry about it. Kick me out of the group if you so desire."*

I thought the planned response would do the trick. If I were kicked out of the group, then I would no longer have to come to meetings like this and 'welcome' child molesters. And then I lied again as I spoke to Paul.

"Welcome to Celebrate Recovery," I lied. "Glad you are here," I lied.

"Are you David? Curt said that I should meet some guy named David."

I finally spoke the truth and admitted I indeed was David, had been David for quite a long time, and planned on being David for a time yet to be determined. I do not want to give the impression that I had suddenly turned noble – my *"Hello My Name is David"* name tag pinned on me gets most of the credit for the current honesty surge.

Paul then spoke. He spoke for about fifteen minutes. He told me his story. Years ago, he had indeed molested his two stepdaughters. He had lived in darkness for most of his life. When one of his victims charged him with the crime, committed twenty years earlier, he denied nothing. In fact, he admitted more. He was sick of the darkness, for it was the darkest of all darkness.

In every moment, darkness consumed him. When the dam broke, he was glad. And his sins flooded everyone in its path.

The path of destruction from this flood was evident everywhere. His wife of forty years divorced him. His children and grandchildren disowned him. The court orders stated he must stay far away from them. He will probably never see any of his family again. And he knows this is fair, and doesn't argue against it.

"I deserve whatever they do to me. I deserve to die for what I did. I blame no one but myself. My hearing is in two weeks, and I will probably spend the rest of my life in jail. Anything less would be a miscarriage of justice. I will and have admitted to everything. I will hide nothing any longer. Light is so much better than darkness."

Paul said more. He said it better than I just wrote it. He said it with no pretense or excuses. He said it with tears, but not those contrived tears some say before a jury and a judge. No, it was just Paul and I, alone on a Friday night.

Then he paused, looking me over to see what my response would be. He knew nothing of my story, how people like Paul turned my stomach. But he was so honest, and I was glad, because I knew I could be honest as well, not that I needed much encouragement.

"Paul," I began, "I must be honest with you also. I do not like people like you. In fact, I am struggling to simply stay here and look at you. One of my children, years ago, was abused. His childhood was stolen from him. I struggle with forgiving the one who did this, and I struggle with forgiving myself for not protecting my son."

I said more, but quite frankly I do not remember exactly what I said. But a strange feeling washed over me as I spoke. I was not harsh enough with him, I thought. There was no yelling or cursing. Yes, I was brutally honest with my feelings, but somewhat amazed that I found myself not hating him.

There is a part of me that must defend the innocent. I imagine that most of us feel this way. I have been taught that when one is a victim of abuse, and they tell you, you need to believe them, defend them, and protect them. It is actually good to act angry with the perpetrators, to say things such as, "I would like to beat the crap out of them." Most would agree it is *not* the right thing to, in any way, defend the abuser or even act kindly or understandable to the abuser, or of course to blame the abused.

So, as I stood there that Friday night talking with Paul, I found myself actually almost feeling something good about him. The feeling began to overwhelm me that I was betraying my own child. Obviously, that is not a feeling I want following me around.

So now, I concluded, I had another issue to discuss in the group that night.

Paul asked if he could stay for Celebrate Recovery. He had no intention of causing anyone any more pain. He would leave if I asked him. He would understand, he told me, if no one wanted him around. He was guilty, guilty as charged, he said. The good thing was that in two weeks he would not be around any longer. He would be in jail.

And then it happened. Jesus became real, perhaps as real as he had ever been to me. Jesus jumped out of heaven and came right to where Paul and I were standing. He made no announcement of his coming. Without question he came into our presence. For I could never hug a child molester, even a repentant one who had gone years without acting out, and who had confessed all of his sins. Even one who appeared genuinely remorseful, and who would be safely locked up for the rest of his life, never to harm another child again.

But for a good two to three minutes, a flawed father who had failed to protect his child years earlier, who had struggled with an intense hate of the one who had stolen his child's innocence; who had yelled at the other father, the perfect Abba Father for not protecting his child; who had questioned the reality of the very

God he preached – that flawed, failed father stood embracing and loving an admitted, soon to be convicted and sentenced abuser, both weeping, and both seemingly not wanting the embrace and the tears to stop soon.

Yes, Jesus did show up that night. He was the hugger. The one called David could never have hugged the one called Paul. Never. But Jesus could. And Jesus did.

A Second Visit With Paul

While we were yet (in the very act of sinning) sinners, Christ died for us.

Romans 5:8, (NIV parentheses mine)

Paul and I had a nice visit the other day. The meeting occurred in a prison that houses only sexual offenders. Paul has been sentenced to eighteen years, being convicted of abusing his stepdaughters. Paul, seventy-two, is glad the truth is out and is paying dearly for the horrific sins he has committed. None who know the story has or would defend him, for the trauma and destruction he has leveled on his victims are indescribable. Nor do I, or will I, defend him.

I visited Paul for a couple of reasons. First, I love Paul, but my love for Paul is tough for me. One I love with all my heart was abused as a child. My acceptance of Paul feels as if I am betraying one of my children. I am a sinner for sure, imperfect in many ways. But I shall never, at least knowingly, betray any of our children. I could not live another day if I betrayed them.

But Paul *did* betray his children and his wife. And he lives to this day. Now I am really confused. So tell me again why I visited Paul? Oh yes, I love him.

The love and compassion I feel for Paul should not be confused with God's love; yet it cannot be understood apart for God's love. The comparison with God's *unconditional* love falls short, for I love Paul *conditionally*. Imagine if the following happened: I meet Paul, and he has a smirk on his face. He tells me he is guilty of nothing and that his victims asked for it, that they somehow provoked or enticed him. He tells me that not only does he not deserve jail-time, but that he has beaten the system. His father has big money, has hired the best attorneys, and he has been acquitted.

In addition, imagine if one of Paul's victims is one of our daughters, and years after the abuse, and because of the abuse, she developed a drug addiction, has three failed marriages, and ended her life by suicide, leaving three young children alone in this world. Would I be writing this today describing a nice visit with Paul because I love him? I do not even have to answer that, do I?

No, I do not love Paul unconditionally. When someone says that there is a vast gulf between God and us, somehow this illustration works for me. I get it. God's love compared to my love is no contest. The comparison is really a contrast. Vast gulf indeed. Yet God told us that we are capable of loving as he loved us, unconditionally.

"While we were still sinners, Christ died for us" (Romans 5:8).

But I do love Paul. And he has done terrible things. How did I get here, sitting at a table in Malvern, Arkansas, staring at this old man in a white jump suit, and then hugging him and crying with him and praying with him?

I am here because of God's love. I have never abused a child, but I have abused God's Son. I have ignored him, questioned him, disobeyed him, and for most of my life have hurt him. I have not really taken him seriously. He has died for me. I have considered his death and at times laughed at it. I have tried to run away from him, hoping to somehow lose him. *If I go here,* I have reasoned, *perhaps he will not show up. If I act as if he does not exist, if I reason enough to prove he indeed cannot exist, then he certainly will not appear again, hanging on the cross with his hands outstretched, blood and loving dripping down.*

But even though I have run many thousands of miles away from him, every single day when I awake, I see him, still there, with arms outstretched to me. He never really goes away. He does love me unconditionally. And I confess, with the exception of our children and grandchildren, and my wife, I do not believe I have ever loved anyone unconditionally, much less him. I feel as if I have not reached my potential. How about you? Think we have more work to do before he comes back?

Romans 5:8 will not leave me alone: "While we were yet sinners, Christ died for us." At the very moment I acted as if his death meant nothing to me, he died for me. On the same day I mocked him and laughed at his prescription for how I should live, he died for me. He died for me, David Mathews. I know he died for you also, and for billions of others, but until I really believed and accepted the fact that he died for the one 't' and non-band guy, \, *me*, did my life ever change.

So I have done a noble thing: I have loved Paul, a convicted, rotten scoundrel of a human. When I tell the story of the night I hugged him, audiences react as if I am really something. Now you know that I am not anything, compared to him who is everything. His love swallows mine whole.

Paul, why? Why did you do what you did? I have to know. I need to understand. I struggle with the one who hurt my child. I want to forgive, but the perpetrator has done nothing to earn my forgiveness. I battle my own demons. What did I do or not do to protect my child? And where is God in all this?

Looking back, perhaps that was too many questions for Paul to answer. After all, humans have been asking similar questions for thousands of years. To my knowledge, though many have attempted to offer answers, few make sense.

Paul's answer was short. "I took my eyes off of God", he said. "I became my own god, and I let evil consume me. But God delivered me out of the darkness, and I have tasted the Light. I will never go back to the darkness. One scripture relentlessly pursues me: 'While I was yet a sinner, Christ died for me.' And that is enough."

Peaks and Valleys

> "You unbelieving generation! How much longer must I be with you? How much longer must I endure you? Bring him to me."
>
> Mark 9:19 (NIV)

Jesus needed a pick-me-up. Father and Son both sensed it. So one day Jesus told his three friends to get their backpacks on and to go with him on a short trip up a mountain. So they did.

Once they arrived at the peak, strange things happened. The significance of that day must be enormous, for two thousand years later we are still talking about it. Most of us know the story. We call it the "Transfiguration." We need to let it transform us.

I can only imagine the drama. Peter helped us capture at least some of the experience by being Peter. When he saw the strange sight of Jesus talking with two men long since dead, but now appearing very much alive, he sputtered his immortal words we laugh at to this day. I am, of course, paraphrasing just a bit.

> Oh, this is really cool. It is so good for us to witness this. Here is Moses and Elijah, two fairly important yet dead people, having a conversation with our Lord Jesus.

> They appear to know one another, and how do I know this is Moses and Elijah anyway? But I do. I am sure of it. Hey guys, pardon the interruption. Yes, I know you must be talking about fairly important issues, but I have a suggestion, if I may? How about if John and James and I build three shelters for you guys? You know the sun is hotter the higher in altitude you go. I, of course, will take the lead in the building. It was my idea, you know.

I have often stated when teaching on this passage that I wish someone would have filmed this entire episode. It would be interesting to see not only what Jesus looked like, but also Moses and Elijah. To see Jesus transfigured might be more amazing than anything these eyes have witnessed. I would have also loved to see the expression on Jesus's face when Peter uttered those words, about the three shelters. "And I picked him to be one of the inner three?" he might be thinking.

Then there was the voice, and no I am not talking about James Earl Jones, though it might have been similar. The voice of God was heard, and it was recorded in writing for us to hear over and over again: "This is my son whom I love him. Listen to him" (Mark 9:7 NIV).

This just might be one of the greatest sermons of all time. And it is slightly shorter than most of my sermons, or for that matter any other sermon in history. Moses and Elijah admittedly had a grand resume, but the Son of God was and is Jesus. "You listen to him," God bellowed. "You listen to him, and all will make sense, including your life."

When they came down the mountain the next day, all four men were feeling pretty good. Jesus had been re-affirmed. God had reminded him of what home was like, what Jesus had left, and what was on the other side of the cross. Being transfigured to the form he originally possessed was better than receiving pictures or videos from home. And Peter, James, and John must have felt more confident in their earlier decision to leave the family's fishing business to follow Jesus. Listen to him? I think so!

As they left the mountain, the real world awaited them. An angry father played the leading role in the drama unfolding below. His son had suffered for years, and the good father was doing whatever he could to find help for his son. When he brought him to the apostles to heal him, they couldn't do it. Nothing worked. The father's high hopes came crashing down. Then he saw his chance. Jesus was finally coming down the mountain.

When the man explained the deep pain of his son, and the apostles' incapability to heal him, Jesus appeared to lose it.

"O unbelieving generation, how long shall I stay with you? How long shall I put up with you? Bring the boy to me" (Mark 9:19).

So they did. In the ensuing conversation, Jesus asked the father about the boy. The father ended his description of the boy's suffering with a passionate plea: "But if you can do anything, take pity on us and help us" (v.22).

Not in the best of moods, Jesus responded quickly and curtly: "If I can? Everything is possible for one who believes" (v.23). Then Jesus healed the boy.

Later, the apostles, with the exception of Peter, James, and John, were understandably embarrassed. They had let down the man, the boy, and their Master. Not a very good day for them. And they had justified Jesus not picking them to go on the mountain trip the day before.

I have a few questions about that episode: Why was Jesus angry with his disciples for not healing the boy, while showing absolutely no anger to his Father? Who had more power, God or the disciples? Who would know just what to do, God or the disciples? Who knew the story of this boy and his dad better than God? I know, I still ask a lot of questions.

Did God not see the suffering of the boy long before he was brought to the apostles? Jesus was angry with his followers because they had the power and the authority to do something about a boy's suffering, but did nothing. And the Son displayed absolutely no anger with his Father, but only toward humans—humans who were just like you and me.

Why so angry, Jesus? Why not ask your Father why he didn't do something about it weeks or months or years ago?

The obvious answers to all the above questions should stun us, convict us, and indeed shame us. To every one of us who has let sin control us, who acts powerless in trying to help others, who has a weak prayer life, who has accepted a mediocre marriage, or has given up the dream of Jesus, who has pity parties more than victory celebrations—to all of us I say look closely at what Jesus was teaching us in that episode. Listen to *him*.

Jesus was saying to all of us *how* God works in this world, then and now. God does his work through *people* who *believe*, not through people who are well-trained, smart enough, or good enough. "Everything is possible for him who believes" (v.23). God, it appears, was not to blame for this boy's suffering; the disciples were to blame.

Jesus was once again affirming what God has long tried to teach us, namely that each human being has incalculable worth, value, purpose, and power. Does God need us for God to accomplish his will on this earth? He apparently did here. We were created to make positive, life-saving impact on people. Jesus and we are meant to be in the same boat, throwing out lifelines to those drowning in the sea of life. He is the captain of the boat, and without him we can do nothing. But without us, without our believing, God is severely handicapped in what he can do to help people.

I know that sounds a bit arrogant; I understand that it appears to water down God's power, but how else do you explain his anger at humans in this story and his non-anger at God? The high stakes of being human, indeed. Listening to him might be the most important thing I do today, or ever.

What Did God Do Before He Created?

> 14. Behold, I answer to him who asks, "What was God doing before He made heaven and earth?" I answer not, as a certain person is reported to have done facetiously (avoiding the pressure of the question), "He was preparing hell," saith he, "for those who pry into mysteries." It is one thing to perceive, another to laugh,—these things I answer not. For more willingly would I have answered, "I know not what I know not..."
>
> The Letters and Confessions of St. Augustine, Chapter XII

The question apparently was asked with regularity in the early years of Christianity. I imagine it was asked for hundreds, perhaps thousands of years before God became a baby. At first glance, the question appears to have little relevancy. You might be like many of my friends, when hearing yet another one of *those* questions, politely leave my presence to go some place better to do something better than trying to answer one of *those* questions. When Augustine was asked that question, his initial response, referencing someone else, was that God was preparing hell for those who ask such questions.

Before you quote Mr. Augustine or leave, please consider the following scriptures, which tell us plainly what he did before he ever said, "Let there be light."

> Ephesians 1:4 – "For he chose us in him *before the creation* of the world to be holy and blameless in his sight."
>
> Ephesians 3:11 – "According to His eternal purpose which He accomplished in Christ Jesus our Lord."
>
> 1 Peter 1:20 – "He was chosen *before the creation* of the world, but was revealed in these last times for your sake."
>
> 1 Corinthians 2:7 – "No, we speak of God's secret wisdom, a wisdom that has been hidden and that God destined for our glory *before time began.*"

If we take scripture seriously, we can state with confidence that God therefore thought of us before he created. He chose us before he created. He chose Christ before he created, which of course means he planned a way out for us, before he ever created one of us. He decided that his secret wisdom (which revolved around Christ) would be destined for us, indeed for our glory!

Not only that (can we possible take any more?), he chose us to be holy and blameless in his sight. God is quite a dreamer, isn't he?

After looking at these passages and thinking about them, some thoughts entered my mind that I initially dismissed as being too crazy to even repeat to another living human. These thoughts momentarily dazed me. *If true*, I thought, *then everything about my life changes—everything*. I need to be careful here. I tend to exaggerate everything, and I mean everything.

But if Paul and Peter spoke truth, I honestly do not know how anyone could exaggerate the meaning of God thinking of us before time began. I know of few if any who have made too much of this. There is ample evidence that the opposite is true. Most that I know, including me, have not come within miles of making too much of this. Consider the following implication of these scriptures.

GOD HAS NEVER DONE ANYTHING THAT DOES NOT CONCERN US... EVER

This appears to be some kind of a leap, a jump to a conclusion unwarranted by the evidence. I first shared this concept (that God has never done anything without regarding humans) with four trusted friends. About eighty percent of them (3.2) disagreed and begged me to reconsider. It appears quite arrogant, most surmised. But is it? Humor me for a moment.

Assume, just for argument sake, that this might just be true. Here is why I say this. In John 5, when Jesus healed on the Sabbath, a heated discussion broke out between the Jews and Jesus. Jesus defended his action by referring to God as his Father. If my Father works, then I must work. That, of course, rankled the experts of the law, because Jesus had called God his Father, in a sense claiming equality with God.

In verse 19, Jesus astounded them, and us, by pulling back heaven's curtain and letting us see the inner workings of God. "Very truly I tell you, the Son can do nothing by himself; he can do only what he sees his Father doing, because whatever the Father does the Son also does." Verse 20 clinches the claim: "For the Father loves the Son and shows him all he does."

So what does God do all day? What did he do before there was a *day*? The answer is found in looking at Jesus. What did Jesus do? Why did he get up in the morning? Better yet, why did he come to this earth in the first place? Remember, the Father shows the Son *all* that he does, and the Son can only do what he sees the Father doing.

Jesus came for us, because the Father asked him to. Jesus lived on this earth for us. Jesus was determined to be sinless for us. It was the only way—a perfect, sinless sacrifice, bearing our sins. Jesus loved people. He spent time with people. His heart was on fire to show us how great the Father is. Everything he did, and everything he chose not to do, concerned us—us! Jesus prayed, ultimately for us. His ultimate purpose was and is to bring humans made in the image of God back into intimate eternal relationship with God.

In other words, Jesus did nothing that did not concern *us!* If he did only what he saw the Father do, then we know what God does all day, what he has always done.

The one who composed the eighth psalm would agree with the above premise.

> When I consider all that God has made, how big it all is, and then look at humans, why God? Why are you so concerned with us? All that you created was for us, you say. You put us in charge of this wondrous creation, putting everything under our feet. And you made us a little lower than... ?

Many translators hesitate here at verse 5. The word used by David is *elohim.* Of course it means *God*, or it can mean *heavenly being*. God is a heavenly being of course; he is *the* heavenly being. The writer is in awe of the magnitude of God's creation, and when he considers mankind, why would God entrust this creation to us? He created us a little lower than *elohim*, and God crowned us with glory and honor!

Could David be claiming that God created us a little bit lower than God himself? Or should we translate this, as many do, as *angels?* Angels are, after all, heavenly beings as well.

The debate rages about this. Albert Lemmons, who studied every verse of the Hebrew scriptures with Jewish rabbis, shares these thoughts concerning Psalm 8 (in a private correspondence):

> Psalm 8 is David's praise for Divine excellence. He then poses one of earth's most amazing questions: What Is Man? In the creation of man positives outweigh the negatives. Angels do have some super human abilities, but they were not created in the "image and likeness of God" (Genesis 1:26). The English mistranslation of the classic Hebrew text in Psalm 8:5 has many implications. First, the Hebrew word *elohim* is never translated "angel." How or why the LXX did so is inexplicable.
>
> It may well have been that in an eternal occasion of Divine consciousness there was a need for companionship. Out of that came the thought of a creature akin to Himself with intuitive capability with whom He might hold communion. Except man, God created all things with words. Man, he created with his breath (Job 32:8; 33:4). That being the thought of God and in its realization his love and power co-operated and man came into being. Nothing gives such value and dignity than to know that every human is a thought and a breath of God, a product of his love and power[15].

Many translations agree with Dr. Lemmons, and translate 'elohim' in Psalm 8 'God', including the American Standard Version, The Revised Standard Version, the New American Standard Version, the English Revised Version, the Geneva Bible, and others.

Does it matter, one might ask, whether *elohim* is translated "God" or "angel"? There is ample evidence elsewhere in scripture that we are commanded by God to be like God. We are to love as he loved, forgive as he forgave. We are made to participate in the divine nature, the weak, sinful Peter wrote. I have already noted the vast gulf that exists between God and us. We are not God of course. But we are, according to Psalm 8 and really all of scripture, the highest part of his creation. He created us with love in order to love. If "God is love" (1 John 4:8 NIV), and if we are to love as he loves, then we were created to be like God.

What matters is that we see and accept and believe that being human is indeed high stakes. Being human is our identity, for being human is a little lower than God himself. Of course the Creator is higher than those he created. But if the Creator desires that part of his creation be like him, he must create that part with the capabilities to actually be like him. Human beings, David said in Psalm 8, are that part. Believing this does not necessarily make us arrogant, though it certainly can lead us there. The thought that we as humans are that important to God should drive us to our knees in praise of God: "Lord our Lord, how majestic is your name in all the earth" (Psalm 8:1 NIV). As Lemmons concluded,

> If we appreciate the significance of such a thought, that we are God made, in his image and likeness, we would delight in His grace, mercy and love. It would elevate our conception of who we really are. It would dignify our human life. It would deliver us from every wrong motive, from every unworthy thought and ungodly act[16].

So what does it matter one may ask, what God did before He created? To many, the question is irrelevant. But if we really believe we were created a little lower than God himself, we might just begin living with vigor and purpose.

When Augustine seriously attempted to answer the question of what God did before Creation, he said that God did nothing. At the moment God began to create, so the theory goes, time was born. There was no "before this moment" (before Creation), for there was no time. If no time existed, one cannot talk using time terms, such as using the word *before*.

As stated earlier, if one considers "thinking" as "doing," God certainly "did" a lot before he created. He without question thought about us. He planned for us. He visualized us and knew that rebellion would eventually come from free-will creatures who have the capacity to love. Thus in his eternal purpose, he planned for his Son to come to earth and die for our sins, so his justice and holiness could be upheld.

One question: What else would God do? I must admit that God could have possibly done other things, since our knowledge of him is limited. But what else would "Love" (God's definition) do besides love? Would God have a hobby, say playing golf? But after having a thousand or so hole-in-ones, would not that grow old? No, all that God has ever *done* is to love.

Before time began God loved. He was Three in One. Father, Son, and Holy Spirit certainly loved each other. How they demonstrated that love to one another is one of those *unknowables* that we will know only when we get there with them some day. But whatever they did, they loved.

Earlier in this book, we discussed the apparent dilemma of an all-loving, all-powerful God creating a world in which billions would endure horrific pain and live in an endless hell forever. The question of "Why?" is a good question. Why would God go ahead with Creation if he knew the outcome; and why doesn't God take away the pain, and certainly why doesn't he eliminate hell altogether? We need not and should not dismiss the question of why lightly. God created us with minds that ask questions. He told us that if we seek we will find. In the book of Job, God appeared upset with Job's friends, for they had not spoken of God in a right way.

I believe part of the answer is to understand God's dilemma. The other parts that we simply cannot get will be understood when we see him face to face. The answer that at least helps me, and I hope and pray helps others, is that creation of humans with the capacity to love (and thus to not love) flowed out of the heart of God as naturally as his breathing. Had he not created humans to love and from whom to receive love, God would have stopped breathing! And that of course is impossible, for the Infinite One cannot die. It bothers many of us to think of God as being forced to do something. It is as if God is weak, and thus not all-powerful.

But actually it is quite the opposite. God is forced to love by his own love. That forcing is not against his will; no, it *is* his will, for he is love. The *forcing* is not from some stronger outside force. No, it comes from within him. It is, as I said earlier, a sign of the strength and power of his love, and not a sign of any weakness whatsoever.

Remember, God's wisdom is foolishness to us. Creating humans with the capacity to say yes or no to him, and thus opening up the reality of a fallen world (and with it all the pain and suffering), flows out of God's wisdom. The power that love possesses is thus almost incomprehensible. The fact that we are here, that humans exist, is an indisputable testimony that it is wiser and better to exist, thus having the opportunity to have an intimate relationship with the Creator, than to not exist.

The decision God made to create comes out of one thing only—his love. There is no way to totally understand that point here on this earth. But we can understand some of it, indeed enough of it. God must love, thus he creates. He knows the problems associated with our being created. So before he created, he planned our salvation. Father and Son and Spirit discussed the only solution. The Son had an eternity to think about the day the sun stood still for three hours, as did the Father and the Spirit. I understand a little more why he cried out in a loud voice, "It is finished!" (John 19:30 NIV). It had been a long time coming.

Although we cannot possibly know all there is about God's activities before he created, this we know for sure: God's only Son was sent to this earth for us, he lived for us, and he died for us. Jesus was shown everything God was doing (John 5) and Jesus did those things he saw the Father doing. And all that Jesus did concerned us. Every single thing.

GOD GIVES US EVERYTHING WE NEED TO HAVE THIS RELATIONSHIP

The second implication for God thinking of us before time began should be quite obvious. Paul in Romans 8 says as much. My paraphrase: Look, God gave us his only Son, to die for us and to save us. If someone, anyone, gives up their most prized possession for us, such as a Son, don't you know that they will give us anything else that we might need? No super intelligence needed to understand that, right?

Add this to that line of thinking: if *all* God ever does is to pursue us, to provide all that we need, so that we may have an eternal relationship with him, then what are the odds that we can truly have that relationship? It really is up to us to accept it, to access the gift. God has desired and planned this for an eternity. He has had enough *time* to work out his plan, and to work out any kinks. He certainly would not have created anything until every detail of the plan was devised. Jesus coming to earth and saving us was not some compulsive act of God.

What might this mean to those daring enough to simply say, "Okay, if God is on our side, then what? What becomes of our sin struggle, you know the one we simply cannot whip? What happens to our prayer life? How might we respond differently to bad news, even really bad news?" And, thus, the third implication.

ALL THE BAD, ALL THE UNEXPLAINABLE, ALL THE INJUSTICES MAKE SENSE

We have said that God has been working on this plan for an eternity—before time began. That means he has had plenty of time to get it right, since there was no time yet. Now my brain is beginning to hurt again.

But think about it: God must exist; therefore we must exist. We were created to be with God forever. Do you think that God would go to all the trouble to create us if this is not consistent with his very being? Hasn't his workload been increased since Creation? We have claimed, all right I have claimed, that we are his only workload. *We* are what God does.

DEATH IS AN ACT OF GRACE

If that is true, then God in his infinite wisdom has decided that it is possible for us to *get* it. He created us with that capability. It is C.S. Lewis's "homesickness." It is why this world does not satisfy us. We were created for eternity. Thus the physical can never fully satisfy. "So quit trying to find fulfillment in the created things," God cries. "You *all* were made for *me*.

So bad stuff happens, to everybody—stuff so hurtful that at times it knocks us to the canvas. We find ourselves cut and bleeding, staggering to make it to the corner before the ref counts to ten. "God confuses us, if there is a God," we shout.

Over and over again, from life's experiences to stories in the Bible, God sends one dominant theme: I do not value life on this fallen planet as you guys do. I hate it when you hurt. "In this world you will have trouble," Jesus said in John 16:33. But he adds the clincher, "but take heart, I have overcome the world."

Jesus implied that he knows that there are times when he is simply powerless to stop all our pain on this earth. People have the power to choose, and so often their choices hurt others. He is saying that although he cannot stop all of this on this earth, he promises us, in essence it has already been stopped. All pain, all tears, all confusion and fear, all apparent defeats have been blown away by his Son.

Thus, all that happens on the earth, from free-will sins of others and of us, to disease, natural disasters, and accidents—all that happens can be used to increase heaven's population. Heaven's population being increased is all that is on God's to-do list.

GOD IS INDEED A REALLY BIG BIG GOD—BIG ENOUGH

Our fourth child is Chuck. His real name is Charles Richard Mathews. But Chuck really is Chuck, because Charles is much too Charles-y.

We adopted Chuck when he was a little over a year old. His entrance into our world came with quite a bit of humor. Chuck's biological mother is white. His biological father is black. When we were in the process of the adoption, we gathered our other three children together for one of those infamous family meetings. We explained how their new brother was half-black and half-white. Kelly, two at the time, looked a bit puzzled, much more than normal. "Daddy," she sincerely began, "Which side of him is white, and which side is black?"

As Chuck became part of our lives, being the bi-racial son we had never had, he appeared a bit apprehensive of his new parents and siblings. Thus, he shared a room with his big brother, who loved and protected him, as a big bubba should.

One day, we moved into a new house that provided a bedroom for each of the kids. Three of the four were excited. Chuck was petrified. He had never been alone in his own room with the darkness and the monsters lurking.

When I put him to bed that first night, fear dominated him. As a good dutiful daddy, I assured him that he would not be alone. Mommy and Daddy were right across the hall.

"But Daddy, the monsters are in the room with me. And those monsters are bigger than you and Mommy."

Of course I, having a master's degree in theology, brilliantly responded that God was in the room with him, and he was quite capable of dealing with the invisible monsters. "God is bigger than all the monsters in the world," I told him.

"Daddy, how big is God? If he is bigger than all the monsters, he must be really big. How big is he, Daddy?"

Please remember, before judging my response, that Chuck was five or six, so my response needed to be simple enough for him to understand, but deep enough to impress him with the enormity of God. However, I do believe I choked.

"Well, let's see, Chuck. I believe that God is... really big."

"But how big, Daddy? Is he bigger than 487 tall buildings?"

"Yes, Chuck. God is bigger than 487 tall buildings. I think you got it. That's pretty big, isn't it?"

"Yes, Daddy. That's big enough."

So Chuck went to sleep, confident that his God was big enough. Indeed he is. Before the creation of the world, God thought of us, and how he would protect us from all those monsters. He is also bigger than all the dirt in the world.

Every 52 Seconds

> Women speak 250 words per minute versus the 125 words a minute that are typical for men. A woman uses 20,000 words per day, while a man uses only 7,000. Men think about sex every 52 seconds, while women tend to think of it just once a day.
>
> —Dr. Louann Brizendine,
> "The Female Brain"

One day in the mid-sixties, Kip and I were sitting at the Houston Astrodome, getting ready to sell popcorn to the masses (we were both vendors). We discussed what all teenage boys discuss. Kip was trying to figure out if following Christ was possible.

"Why is it so difficult, if not impossible, to wait for marriage before having sex? I try every day to be pure, but I must admit it is not working. I can think of nothing else besides sex. Why doesn't God make it a bit easier?"

Now I was a couple of years older than Kip, which might explain why he was asking me these questions. He foolishly thought my two extra years of living had enlightened me in the sexual realm. The only thing those two extra years did was make me two years more frustrated and confused than Kip.

"I have no idea," I intelligently responded. "I guess it is *supposed* to be difficult."

Ask any group of believers if living for God is easy or difficult, and the vast majority would say, "Of course" (meaning *both*), but definitely they would be leaning toward the "difficult" extreme. Most would assume the reason is because God wants it that way.

But does he? Does God really want us to think the whole idea of being a true follower of Christ is only for a select few who can do it? That most of us have no chance of making it?

In the original Earth, called the Garden of Eden, the first two people had the balance tilted heavily toward the good side. At first, every tree but one was available (God added another forbidden tree, after the fall, see Genesis 3:22). They could eat all they desired, whenever they wanted, from all kinds of trees. Only one was prohibited. I would have loved those odds. In God's original plan, all details were calculated. There simply must be something that is *possible* for Adam and Eve to do, but at the same time be *forbidden*. The forbidden tree is described as the tree of the knowledge of good and evil. For us to have even the possibility of loving, we must have the choice not to love.

In creating this perfect world for us, God could not cheat. Had he made the forbidden tree one of slimy, crawling, awful-tasting creatures, there would not be much of a choice involved. It would be like my father saying, "David, you can have all the steak and ice cream and cookies that are in the house, but do not touch or eat that rotten possum." *Not* eating that would not prove my love and would actually be no choice at all.

No, the choice was a real choice and had to involve the very core of our being. Satan is the father of lies. Great lies are filled with truth. There had to be choice, real choice. And this knowledge of good and evil filled the prescription perfectly.

Why would two people, who had plenty of food, as much as they wanted, and whenever they wanted, with the greatest cook around, eat of something the cook warned them not to touch? The answer just might be the paradox of all paradoxes.

Humans are created from the heart of God—to be loved by God and to love God in return. Coming from the very breath of God, we exist to become like him, to love as he does, forgive as he does, and the like. Made in his image, we by nature have a desire for eternity within us. We yearn for connection with our Creator and are never satisfied until that connection is realized. Satan, knowing that, seizes on this "image of God" truth and plays it accordingly: "Eat of the forbidden tree," he whispers, "and you will be like God. And this is what he does not want. He really does not have your best interests at heart."

Humans are higher than all of God's other creatures. There is a high price for being human with high expectations and high rewards. With that naturally comes the other side. It is called pride. Satan succumbed to it; all humans battle it. We have a taste of the divine, and we want more. If we are not careful, the desire is easily tipped to the side of pride. We want to be God—our own God—and then we want to become God to other humans as well. Power corrupts, so they say. *They* are right.

"Go ahead and eat. You will be glad you did," Satan says. And we are for a while, but isn't it strange that all that eating leaves us starving to death?

Sparkin'

> "I tell you the solemn truth, unless a kernel of wheat falls into the ground and dies, it remains by itself alone. But if it dies, it produces much grain."
>
> John 12:24 (NIV)

"Do you remember when Debbie and you were sparkin'?" His question caught me off guard. Not only did I not know what sparkin' meant (I now know; my wife has informed me that I am one of the few people in the world who does not know what sparkin' means), but I really wasn't paying attention. He looked terrible, as if he was dying, because he was. As he spoke, I thought that one day that would be me.

I had not seen him much in the last few years. He was a member of a church where I worked as a summer intern in the early seventies.

The word from the doctor was not good: *cancer,* perhaps a couple of months to live. His son had asked my wife if I was coming into town in the next few weeks, and if so, could I come to see him. "It would make his day," he told my wife. So the next day, I made the two-hour drive to see an amazing man for the last time.

He was just as I expected, sitting in an easy chair with a blanket wrapped around him up to his chin. He was also asleep. "Let's wake him up," his wife said. "He will be so glad to see you."

I was not looking forward to the visit. Talking to a dying seventy-eight-year-old man usually does not make it on my to-do list, for obvious reasons. It would not have mattered had he been younger. The key word that takes the fun out of the visit is *dying*, not *seventy-eight.*

Some words simply do not sound good. *Death* is one of those. I do not understand a lot about this subject. I know I do not like death, mostly because it tends to sneak up on you and grab you before you're ready. The unfair thing about death is that you do not know when you are going to get it. If you could know the approximate date when death decides to make an appearance, like May 7, 2040, then perhaps you could take it better, unless you were born in 2030.

But he knew. The signs were evident. Cancer, the doctor's prognosis, old friends suddenly dropping by, women giving up their seats for him, everyone speaking in a whisper around him, and a wife who for months had been sick herself suddenly getting better to take care of him. It mattered not that he knew it was coming; death still was unfair, and he did not like it.

The next hour talking to a dying man ranks up there with the great hours of all my life—one hour when an old country man taught me about death, but really about life.

I had heard for years through various sources that you cannot get a handle on life until you grab hold of death. Once the idea of death is looked in the eye, it releases one to begin living. Let death hound you and control you, chances are that life might be out of control. Understanding the relationship between these two can be quite simple. There is no death without life, and no real life until death occurs. Seems like a carpenter's boy said something like that once. "Don't you know," he said shortly before he died, "that for a seed to live, it first has to die?" (See John 12). And another time, he told those willing to listen, "If you want to experience real life, try dying, and see how much more alive you feel" (See Matthew 16).

It took a conversation with a dying man for me to see the truthfulness of those words of Jesus and to understand more fully Peter's words in John 6:68, "Lord, to whom shall we go? You have the words of eternal life."

If you are expecting a report on how this man I visited was cheerful and full of courage as he faced death, you might be disappointed. He was scared, no doubt about it. He also cried a lot, as it seemed any good memory set him off. But there was a strange power in the words he spoke that day, words that I can still hear thirty years later. When he finished, I felt more alive than I had for years.

"I'll never forget it," he continued. "You and Debbie were sparkin', and we had that church picnic, remember? I was sitting all alone at this table, and Debbie and you sat down with me and started talking to me. I don't guess I will ever forget that. Do you remember that, David?"

I remembered nothing about any church picnic, or about talking to L.F. Simmons that day, but I remembered a lot about Debbie and me sparkin'. Even though lying is not something I like to admit, and what I said was a bit deceptive, I must be truthful. I would probably do it the same way again.

"Mr. Simmons, I don't think I will ever forget that day either." And I haven't.

So he talked, and I mostly listened. Do you know what we talked about? Sure you do. He talked about life, real life. Do you know what he didn't talk about? Sure you do.

Let's see. He never mentioned the cars he owned, his bank accounts, his investments, or any of his possessions. He didn't appear to be concerned with the clothes he wore, the house that needed painting, or the carpet that needed replacing. He never came close to lamenting the people in his life that had wronged him. Never did he bring up all of life's disappointments or the bad breaks he had endured. To listen to him, you would think he never had a bad day.

He talked a lot, about people. He began, not surprisingly, with his wife and what a blessing she had been. "David, she has been sick for weeks, but when the doctor said I got this cancer, she suddenly got better. She's just been wonderful." He then proceeded to speak of his two children, Laymon Hankins and Billy Edward. "Two fine boys. I am so proud of them." He never complained about how bad they had been, what a hassle they were, how they left his tools outside, the doors open, or the lights on. He told me how in 1946 he and the two "young 'uns" had built a barn together. He and his boys hammered every nail. You would have thought they built Yankee Stadium to hear him describe it.

Then he started on his grandchildren. It was at that point I realized I was going to be there for a while longer. He took them in the order of their birth, beginning with the oldest. He gave their full names. Every grandchild was his special one. The word *proud* was used on each of them. For a time there, I thought I was talking to a Kennedy or a family of royalty.

Then he pointed out that he had worked for the railroad for over forty years, "With the finest people on God's good earth." He showed me items in his living room that had been gifts from special friends, describing in detail the context of each. They reminded him of the good ole days, and the laughter and the tears flowed on together.

After we said our goodbyes and hugged for the fifth time, it dawned on me how this life and death mix works. L.F. Simmons was in control of death. It was tossing him about, and it hurt. But the important thing was that death was not controlling him. He didn't like it, but strange as it sounds, I truly thought that he had it whipped. For as we talked, I couldn't help but notice how life words filled the air. In the midst of death, a man was talking life—people, love, and family. He never used a self-centered word, and nothing about those things that do not matter.

You see, life reigned in L.F. Simmons, because he had long ago died. His life was constantly involved with others, and part of him, most of him, was in all those he had loved.

As I was about to leave, there was one other he had to tell me about. He was their only great-grandchild. To hear him talk, Dusty was the only great-grandchild in the world. As I viewed Dusty's picture, I saw a spark of my dying friend in that boy, a spark that had life written all over it.

I finally left after an hour or so. Tears filled my eyes as I drove out of their gravel driveway. I promised myself I needed to be more like him and to realize the really important things in life. I vowed to hug my wife and kids a little more and to say a few more prayers of thanksgiving for the blessings of life.

I had a conversation with death, and life showed up. And I discovered what sparkin' was all about.

One and Seventeen

> This is truly, beyond measure, a warm and hearty prayer. He opens the depths of His heart, both in reference to us and to His Father, and He pours them all out. It sounds so honest, so simple; it is so deep, so rich, so wide, no one can fathom it.
>
> —Martin Luther

L.F. Simmons died a few weeks after he changed my life with a one-hour, one-sided conversation. That experience taught me to listen to dying people, at least to people who know they are dying. One does not have to have a doctor's grim prognosis to realize death is coming. But when one does have the official pronouncement of death, listening to them might be a very good thing to do.

Though this might sound somewhat morbid, I have grown to love talking to those who are in their right mind and who are about to leave this world. (You could possibly say that, until you really believe that you were born to *leave this world*, you cannot truly be in your "right" mind.) On each of those occasions when I was privileged to be there, life became more alive and death more real, which in turn enriched life.

The other day I re-visited my favorite chapter of scripture, John 17. The thought came to me that if words spoken by a dying person were so profound and life giving, what about prayers of a dying Savior? Could they possibly be even more profound and life changing? Try reading John 17 reflectively, slowly, and even prayerfully, and see what you think.

On a day in history a man prayed to his God. Many have called this prayer the greatest prayer ever recorded. Of course ranking prayers borders on insanity. How does one decide what prayers make the top ten? I remember others' prayers about as often as people remember my sermons. That means that I can recall about 1.3 prayers I have heard.

Three thoughts make the prayer of Jesus in John 17 memorable. The one who prayed is Jesus. The date of the prayer is around two thousand years ago. The setting of the prayer is in the shadow of the cross, the darkest day in history, yet perhaps the greatest.

There were three men a short distance from Jesus as he prayed that night. One could assume that they perhaps heard portions of the prayer, but there is no evidence that they had pen and paper in hand taking notes. However, there is ample evidence that these three were fearful and were struggling to stay awake. Yet two thousand years after he prayed, we can know the very words the Son of God cried out to his Father that night.

Other observations make that prayer more astonishing. The one who said the prayer had claimed to be God. Thus we have one who claimed to *be* God praying *to* God. Also, the one who claimed to be God was about to die. The prospect of my God dying does not compute in this brain. I prefer that God be alive than dead for many reasons.

So we had God praying to God before God died two thousand years ago, with the words he prayed preserved for the world to read at any time in whatever language that is familiar. Jesus was facing what he had planned throughout eternity. He had probably had nightmares concerning the cross. His soul was "overwhelmed" he had told the three disciples. Yet we are privileged to eavesdrop on those intimate words spoken by an obedient yet fearful Son, mere hours away from the most pivotal day in history. What is it that God wants us to learn?

As we know, Jesus was born to die. God planned his entrance into our physical existence so, among other things, he could die not only physically but also spiritually. He allows us to enter into his most intimate thoughts as the dreaded hour approaches. We know what he is feeling, fearing, facing. God has no intention to hide truth, of wearing the masks we as humans seem determined to wear. God majors in intimacy, which in one sense petrifies us, while at almost the same moment inspires us to heights we never dreamed.

John 17 is essentially about intimacy: intimacy between the Father and his Son, between his Son and us, and then between others and us. That just might be crucial for all our relationships, including but not restricted to husbands and wives, other relatives, friends, and even our relationship to the junk and the pain of this world. Tied together with all these relationships is our connection to the One who created us. We spend our lives trying to see him, find him, and understand him. His actions, non-actions, silence, and expectations confuse us and at times leave us numb.

We try everything available to find true, lasting meaning to this thing we call life. There are moments when I absolutely know that God does not love me, care for me, or even think about me. None of it makes sense. But then he seems to appear out of nowhere, showing up in all the unexpected places. In moments like those, I am absolutely positive he knows my name, that Mathews has only one 't' in it, and that I have a pointed head.

Josiah was born on October 3, 2007, in the same hospital where his daddy was born twenty-nine years earlier. We had not lived in that city for sixteen years, but life led our son and his wife back to the city of his birth. As my wife and I entered that hospital and went to the fourth floor, memories flooded us both. In the same place where we experienced the indescribable joy of our firstborn coming into our lives, we were about to experience the indescribable pain of watching our son and his wife hold their firstborn until he died.

When the extended family went into the delivery room, we each were honored to hold Josiah and say our hellos and goodbyes. I did not expect to find God there; I hate to admit it, I am not sure I *wanted* to meet God there. But we not only met him there, we hugged him there. Intimacy is indeed worth taking off our dumb masks. It is the only way to live.

Heroes Take Pictures

All heroes are shadows of Christ.

—John Piper – *Don't Waste Your Life*

It was the day of our grandson's birth... and death. Friends and family had gathered to offer their love, prayers, hopes, and support. The waiting room was full. I knew most of the people there, except for one couple sitting quietly with cameras around their necks. Our son wanted us to meet them. "Dad, talk to them. You will be glad you did."

So we did. Their story didn't take long to share, but its impact has and will inspire many for a long time.

They'd had five children, all of whom had died. They were professional photographers and were fulfilling their mission. For years, they had been quietly going about their work of taking pictures of babies and their families when the doctors thought the baby would never leave the hospital alive. And then if the family wanted the disc of pictures, they gave it to them, totally free of charge. No charge for their time; no charge for anything.

So that's what happened. Josiah was born, and shortly thereafter he died. The extended family was escorted into the delivery room, where we took turns holding a precious little boy. We cried and hugged each other, and gently touched Josiah David.

And as we mourned, a couple with the deep scars and the unbearable pain in their hearts from losing five children went about taking picture after picture. We hardly noticed them there. They were good at what they did.

After about thirty minutes, we left the room so Josiah could be alone with his mother and father. We passed the couple and said the obvious thank you. They acknowledged our feeble attempts to say the right thing.

Funny thing, I did not have to ask them why they did what they did. No one did. We all knew. They did it because they had to.

Years ago, I had defined a hero as "someone who could play a game better than most." My first hero was Eddie Mathews, a baseball player from the 1950s and '60s. He was my hero because our last name was the same, and when I first met him he acted as if I was important to him. I got his autograph seven times. Each time I saw him over the years, I am convinced he remembered me. He was a really good hero.

I never got my new heroes' autographs, at least not in the traditional sense. I got much more than that. In our room, we have beautiful pictures of a little boy. And every time I look at them, which is every day, I think of a couple with cameras hanging around their necks. Those are the autographs I will always keep.

In-To-Me-See (And Still Love Me)

Our souls crave intimacy.

—Erwin Raphael McManus, *Soul Cravings*, p. 9

Intimacy is difficult to define. When we experience true intimacy, once we get passed the initial fear and shock, we know more about it and like it. It helps life become... life. We feel alive. Yet even after we become intimate with intimacy, we still struggle to put it into words.

Once I heard someone define *intimacy* as "In-To-Me-See." I would add "And-Still-Love-Me." I like that. Basically, when someone knows the real me, and accepts me and loves me just as I am, that's intimacy. Of course, there are many levels of this challenging word.

Jesus in his prayer recorded in John 17 longs to be back with the One with whom he is the most intimate. His father knows everything about him. "And now, Father, glorify me in your presence with the glory I had with you before the world began" (John 17:5 NIV).

This is indeed a long, long relationship. Earlier in his prayer, recorded in Mark 14, Jesus did something extraordinary. He shared with three flawed humans that he was overwhelmed with sorrow to the point of death. Then he asked them to help him, "Sit here while I pray" (Mark 14:42 NIV).

Then on his knees Jesus asked his Father to take the cup from him, even though he most certainly knew the forthcoming answer. Then why pray the prayer? Because he was being honest with his feelings to the One he knew would love him, no matter what. Jesus knew the futility of hiding anything. He and the Father had had a long time to work things out. They knew each other. They defined *intimacy*. After all, it is God's idea.

The John 17 prayer is for humans, both then and now. That astounds me, as the Son is about to endure the cross. He began to pray for his apostles, and then for us. His prayer for us is summed up in this: "that all of them may be one, Father, just as you are in me and I am in you" (John 17:21 NIV).

Adam was alone. God was not enough for Adam, so God in his wisdom created a companion. "That is why a man leaves his father and mother and is united to his wife, and they become one flesh" (Genesis 2:14 NIV).

Paul said that was a great mystery (see Ephesians 5), but he was talking about Christ and his church. Oneness again. "Just as a body, though one, has many parts, but all its many parts form one body, so it is with Christ" (1 Corinthians 12:12 NIV). I once thought God's favorite number was seven. Now I believe it is one.

No, It's You, Ray

> Ray, people will come Ray. They'll come to Iowa for reasons they can't even fathom. They'll turn up your driveway not knowing for sure why they're doing it. They'll arrive at your door as innocent as children, longing for the past. Of course, we won't mind if you look around, you'll say. It's only $20 per person. They'll pass over the money without even thinking about it: for it is money they have and peace they lack. And they'll walk out to the bleachers; sit in shirtsleeves on a perfect afternoon. They'll find they have reserved seats somewhere along one of the baselines, where they sat when they were children and cheered their heroes. And they'll watch the game and it'll be as if they dipped themselves in magic waters. The memories will be so thick they'll have to brush them away from their faces. People will come Ray.
>
> —Terrance Mann in *Field of Dreams*

The other night my favorite movie was on TV yet again. Even though I can recite most of the lines, and I have the movie on VHS and DVD, I paused to watch the ending. I cannot stop myself. It still grabs me and tugs on my heart.

I remember the first time I saw it. Just my wife, me, and another couple. The kids were somewhere else, I suppose with someone else, doing something else. When the movie ended, we went home, and I immediately found our oldest child, at that time an eleven-year-old son. Grabbing his baseball glove, I told him nothing else mattered in the world at that time. He and I were going to have a catch. So we did.

When his first throw hit my glove, I paused and looked at the ball, and I thought that there were a limited number of times I would have that experience. And secretly, I thanked Kevin Costner and that goofy wonderful movie of his, *Field of Dreams.*

It really is kind of corny, isn't it? Long-dead baseball players coming to life in a cornfield in Iowa to once again play the game they had loved. And a farmer risking his new farm to build a baseball field before he knew who or if anyone would play on it. And why would the lead player be Shoeless Joe Jackson of all people?

There are many classic plots and sub-plots through that movie. I am no film critic, but I know when a movie hits a homerun, and *Field of Dreams* most assuredly did, just as the people most assuredly will come, Ray.

After James Earl Jones and his voice disappeared in the cornfield, there were two players hanging around. One was Shoeless Joe, the other an unnamed catcher. Ray was there of course with his wife and daughter, who had been saved from choking by Burt Lancaster, baseball player turned doctor by way of Moses and Judah Ben-Hur.

It really could not get any better than that, could it? (That is for all those over fifty, who can remember.)

And just as Shoeless Joe was about to retire for the night, doing what God only knows in the corn, he turned to Ray and said the line that made *sense* of all the *nonsense:* "No, it's you, Ray."

"It's you, Ray?" That's it? That's the line that sent me scurrying to make it home before dark to play catch with my son?

Of course it is. It is the line of the century. It is the line of most of our lives. We do not rest until we get it. And when we do get it, if we are blessed enough to receive it, life gets sweeter. How sad it is when we miss it.

Ray had had a father. And for whatever reasons, he never played enough catch with him. And Ray knew his life would never be complete until he made it right. He had to have one more catch.

I was watching another show the night I happened upon *Field of Dreams*. It is a game show where contestants have to tell the truth to stay in the game. The contestant was a thirty-something man. After answering a number of questions truthfully, he was asked a tough one: "If your father sent you a plane ticket to fly home to see him, would you go?"

The man looked stunned. He finally stuttered, "Of course I would go." The answer was true, so he stayed in the game.

It was then divulged that he had not seen his father in seven years. And then the host shocked the man by bringing out the estranged father. Tears formed in both men's eyes. The father stood before his son and millions of viewers and asked his son: "Would you forgive me for not being present in your life while you were growing up and forgive me for all those times I hurt you?"

Suddenly, winning a lot of money lacked importance. The son answered almost immediately, "Yes! I forgive you." And two grown men on national TV wept as they hugged each other.

They had one more game of catch.

So there was Ray and John, the father-catcher. Ray's wife flipped on the lights, and father and son were doing what they should have done years earlier. And in the background were hundreds of cars winding their way to a cornfield turned into a baseball field where dreams come true.

"Lord, show us the father and that would be enough for us" (John 14:8 NIV).

Father Power

> And because you are sons, God sent the Spirit of his Son into our hearts, who calls "*Abba!* Father!"
>
> Galatians 4:6 (NIV)

Jesus became human because of his love for the Father. He refused to sin because of his desire to return to the Father. He was tempted to forego the cross, and thus sin, because of his reluctance to enter a realm without the Father. He endured the cross in spite of his sorrow precisely because he wanted to please his Father.

What father would even consider putting his son though such an ordeal? For far too long I have missed the pain of the Father in this drama. Omnipotent Jehovah, Maker of heaven and earth, infinite and holy, holy, holy, not only carefully considered the plan, but also painstakingly executed it. Isaiah 53:10 says that it was the Lord's will to crush him; that God "caused him to suffer." And crush him was what the Father did to his Son, his only Son.

How did God actually go through with it? We can understand *how* he did it when we see *why* he did it. If we can see the why, and see that the why is all tied up in us, perhaps finally, after years of not really believing it, we might just say: "He really does love me. If he did this for me, then how can I not love him?"

I cannot love God in a way that changes my life until and unless I am totally convinced of his love for me. "We love because he first loved us," John wrote (1 John 4:19 NIV). I can be convinced of that by something that occurred in real time, in real history. There was a day, a specific day, in which the love of infinite God, Creator of all, burst upon us. The story of that is *the* story. He is not only the King of kings and the Lord of lords, his is *the* story of all stories.

Why then did God crush his Son, and in reality kill him? Could it be that it was because God has other children, whom he brought into this world? Why has it taken me so long to get it? His devotion to the only begotten Son is obvious. God wept as his boy suffered and died. The sun could not shine for those three hours. He was in so much pain that he had to turn his face away and not look at what was happening. There was no joy in heaven. But if the Son did not die, there could certainly be no joy in heaven either. In fact, it would have been much worse. All of God's other kids would have received the death sentence. He would have lost all of us. He brought us into this world out of the same heart of love that he had for his only begotten Son.

He really does love you and me as much as he loves Jesus!

I know, I know, you may be thinking, *Does he really?* Of course. Go back and sit at the cross for a few more moments. When a Father's love is finally seen and accepted, his children not only rise up to praise him, they are emboldened to be more like him. And life suddenly has meaning, perhaps for the first time.

Recently, I was reminded once again about father power. The other day, a thirty-something woman was crying in my office. Her father had abused her when she was a child. For many years she had religiously worked on her recovery, utilizing counselors, Christian friends, twelve-step groups, and I suppose every method possible. She had not been to a counselor for a couple of years, and I thought she was getting on with a bit of normalcy in her life.

So when this woman sat crying in my office, I asked, "Why the tears? What did he do?"

He had done nothing, she said. Her mom had called and wanted to know if she could come home for Christmas and spend just one night with them. "And you are thinking about doing that? I thought your mom understood the situation; that she knew you really could never go home again? She had indicated that she knew that any meeting would take place on your turf, without the dad being present."

"I thought she did too, but I guess it will not hurt me to give on this," she replied. "I think I can do it, but as the day grows closer, I am having nightmares."

"Then why do it?"

Her answer was simple: "He is still my dad."

I guess it really boils down to this: if my own father does not love and accept me, who can?

Years ago, I conducted a men's class on fatherhood. In the first session, we started with an icebreaker. "Let's start with everyone telling us your name, your father's name, and something special about your dad." I expected most to say something like, "My name is David, my father's name was Thomas; he died in 1993. One special thing about my dad was his kindness. He was and I guess still is the kindest person I have ever known."

So that is how we started. I began, and then we went to the person to my right. The man to my right started out perfectly.

"Well, my name is Robert..." He then paused, became extremely emotional, and could barely get out another word. I knew this guy and would never have described him as the emotional type. Tattooed on his forehead for all to see could have been the words *Don't you even think about hugging me.* Finally, after a few very awkward moments, he stammered "Well, there is really nothing good to say about my father. He left me and my mom when I was three, and I cannot think of anything special about him, except that he was a lousy father."

After several moments of complete silence, no one knew quite what to do. If we had been a women's group, seventeen boxes of tissues would suddenly appear. Most of the guys in this group could not even spell *tissues*. So we did what men do—we sat there with no one moving. Being the leader of the class and all, I brilliantly responded after five minutes or so, "Okay, good start. Next!"

Now some of you might think I am making this up, but the next guy was so emotional that he forgot his own name. "My dad never said that he loved me. I could never please him. I was glad when the SOB died, to tell you the truth. And if I had known that I had to talk about him, I never would have let my wife talk me into taking this #@#$#%$# class."

Needless to say, I never again started a class that way.

The theory "If my dad doesn't love me who can?" has been verified time and time again.

A few weeks after the infamous class described above, I was greeting people at our church service. I met a visiting couple from Alabama. "What brings you guys to Michigan?" I asked.

"My dad and mom are in the nursing home here, and it's my dad's ninetieth birthday. We are going to visit them this afternoon and spend about a week here. You might know them; they used to be members here."

It turned out that I did know them and had visited them in the nursing home on numerous occasions. The old man was one of my favorites—tough and ornery, he always spoke his mind. I liked him because I had the freedom to always speak my mind with him. I was never afraid to do that mainly because he was ninety, deaf, and confined to a wheelchair. I felt safe with him.

The next day, I was in my office when I received a phone call from the son's wife. She was upset. Her husband had suffered a massive heart attack while visiting his father in the nursing home. He was alive, but barely.

When I got to the hospital, I found him awake but unable to talk. His wife talked for him.

"Honey, can I tell David what happened yesterday?"

He nodded yes.

She continued, "Yesterday after we talked to you at church, we went to the nursing home to visit Earl. Ed (her husband, Earl's son) was sitting on the edge of his dad's bed, having a great visit. Suddenly, Ed clutched his chest and collapsed into his dad's arms. Earl, lying there in bed, was holding his son, crying out, "Son, please don't die. I love you, son. I love you. Please don't die!"

"Wow," I intelligently responded. "What a great story."

"Wait," she said, "that's not all the story. You see, that is the first time in Ed's sixty-five years of living that he ever heard his father say, 'I love you.'"

As I turned to look at Ed, there in the midst of tubes in his arms and nose, I saw tears streaming down his face.

Ed died three months later, preceding his father in death by a couple of years. He died happy.

Father power. The theory remains true. And Philip's words ring even truer: "Lord, show us the Father, and that will be enough for us" (John 14:8 NIV).

The Hat, Jack-in-the-Box, and the New Car

David, were you hurt?

—Thomas George Mathews,
Summer, 1965

Cleaning out the closet can be profound. Years ago we found an old golf hat that had belonged to my dad. Years earlier our oldest son had discovered it at his grandparents' house. He had asked my dad if he could have it. And so the hat came home with us.

I do not recall when I first saw Dad in that silly-looking hat. I know it was on the golf course, when he, my brother, and I were about to "tear up the links." Every time we played, he wore that same ole hat.

We came close to throwing it out many times, but each time my throw-it-out-if-we-haven't-seen-it-or-used-it-in-the-last decade wife calmly suggested it, something inside of me said, "No, we'll regret it later if we do." So the hat went back into its hiding place.

Why so special, this old, wrinkled, really kind of ugly hat? I kept asking myself that question every time I saved it. The last time, right after dad died, it all became clear. The hat has a certain kindness woven all through it. It is nothing spectacular. But it is easy-going and laid-back. It almost speaks when I look at it, saying, "Here I am. Nothing fake, just me. Take me this way, or no way at all." And the longer you look at it and study it, the more you grow to like it, and even respect it.

So when I see that old hat, I see Dad. I am reminded of his quiet greatness, gentleness, kindness, and the legacy he left his three children. I think back to a moment in my early teens that convinced me how blessed I was to have him as my daddy.

I was fifteen, had just obtained my treasured driver's license, and was about to go to the famous Jack-in-the-Box for lunch. Dad had just purchased a new Chevy and was out of town in the old car. The new car sat proudly in the driveway, looking as if it were saying, "David, don't even think about sliding behind the wheel and driving me."

In case you have forgotten, fifteen is quite an age. For me, being fifteen, living in a new town, and going to a new school was disastrous. Pimples had declared war on my face about a year earlier. I was in the first year of high school, and I felt ugly and alone. (Yes, you have my permission to feel sorry for me.) Fifteen, the year I ate alone at lunch, walked alone in the halls, sat alone in class, and cried alone at night.

Fifteen—the year Mark Little took my self-esteem down to depths never before reached with an eight-word statement I can now repeat forty-seven years later. I was standing in the hallway waiting for the bell to ring signaling the end of lunch. I wore a crew cut in 1965. The Beatles were exploding on the scene, and by that time most of the guys at Westbury High School in Houston, Texas, were letting their hair grow long; that was everyone except me.

So there I was, standing alone in the hall with my crew cut when Mark Little approached. By that time many students had gathered nearby. Mark, for reasons only Charles Manson could grasp, started staring at my head. He slowly stalked around me, never once taking his eyes off of my head, like a lion circling his prey before pouncing. And pounce he did. Suddenly, he burst out laughing as he pointed at my head. His immortal words are etched somewhere under that crew-cut to this day: "Mathews, you really do have a pointed head!"

The implications of those eight words are indeed staggering. For one thing, Little knew my name. In Westbury High school in 1965, only four, possibly five students knew my name, and one of those was my brother. So the odds of someone in the hall knowing my name were like 750:1. Also, Little's statement implied that others had evidently mentioned the possibility of my having a pointed head.

Finally, it implied that I had a pointed head. I went on to grow my hair longer; Little went on and captured the Most Witty Award for the class of '68. So on the day of the Jack-in-the-Box, my self-esteem wasn't even on radar.

I asked Mom if I could take the brand new car to get some burgers for lunch. It was just down the street, I pleaded, and if she let me drive Dad's car, I would get her one of Jack-in-the-Box's famed tacos. The tacos convinced her.

"Just be *careful*," she warned. "Your father told you not to drive it, and he will be back tomorrow."

So off I went, with thoughts of tacos, burgers, and a brand new car with the sticker still attached. Life was getting a little better for this fifteen-year-old.

To capture the moment, you must understand the Jack-in-the-Box phenomena in Houston in 1965. Both adults and teenagers frequented that fine establishment, and McDonald's was still a few years away. It was the first place I remember that had a drive-thru where you could place your order without getting out of your car.

At this Jack-in-the-Box, as you drove through to pick up your order, you passed through an overhang that was supported by three steel poles, to the driver's right.

It was noon. There were at least twenty cars lined up to order. I placed my order and proceeded to the front. Two cars were in front of me, when suddenly, without warning, the good ole new car ran out of gas. Life was getting back to normal.

As it became apparent that I was not moving, most of the people behind me were getting a little impatient. So me, being the brilliant fifteen-year-old that I was, deducted that the best course of action was to have the woman driving behind me to simply push me to the pick-up window so I could get my order and get out of everyone's way. After all, the mob was turning a bit ugly; their tacos were getting cold.

I looked over my left shoulder with my head hanging out the window and asked the lady behind me to give me a gentle push, letting her know that this was my dad's brand new car.

She reluctantly agreed, realizing correctly that the consequences of something bad happening to the new car could be deadly, definitely for me, and probably for her as well.

So she gently began to push my car with her car. I was looking back to make sure she did not dent the car, and did not notice one small problem. She had pushed my dear father's brand-new-sticker-still-on-the-car Chevy directly into the middle pole. It put a very nice dent in the middle of the right rear door, right below the new car sticker.

The mood of the crowd now turned downright vicious. As they got out of their cars to survey the damage, everyone around heard their shouts and laughter.

"Wow! Look at that. A brand new car wrapped around a pole. You don't see that everyday."

"How could anyone be so stupid to do that?"

"Boy, I would hate to be in that kid's shoes when he gets home."

"Well, he deserves it. Anyone that dumb deserves to get it. If he was my kid, he would be grounded for a month."

"And look. He even has pimples!"

And then one said the words that will live in infamy: "Hey, isn't that the kid with the pointed head?"

After a few people helped me untangle the car from the pole, we pushed the car to a safe place out of the way. Luckily, a gas station was next to the Jack-in-the-Box, so I quickly borrowed a gas can and purchased a gallon of gas.

When I returned to the scene, the cars were backed up almost to the street. People were milling around as if that were a "happening." No one seemed eager to leave to go to another place to eat. I figured it was the lure of the tacos. But friends, years later upon hearing the story, pointed out that the tacos were not really that good. They were a thirsty crowd, with somewhat of a lynch-mob mentality. It was as if there was more to come, and they sensed it. And I did not let them down.

I had, of course, never driven this brand new car before. I had never put gasoline into it. I assumed the place to pour the gas was on the side of the car. I of course assumed incorrectly. So I continually walked around the car holding the gas can, looking for the gas cap. After walking around the car a third time, I realized I would never find it on my own.

Many had gathered around, waiting on their orders and also watching the entire play develop before them. There was no finer entertainment anywhere. So they stayed. Finally, one kind soul broke the tension.

"Hey kid, why don't you look under the license plate?"

So I did, found the gas cap, and proceeded to pour the gas into the tank. When I did, a thunderous applause broke out among the gallery. I nodded in appreciation, trying to laugh at myself and thus prove I was not the loser I really felt like.

The gas can I was using had a long spout. As I was pouring the gasoline into the tank, suddenly the spout broke loose and sprayed gasoline over my entire body from the bottom of my feet to the top of my... pointed head. I was completely drenched with gasoline.

The laughter was now out of control. Not one person offered a napkin, water, or even a kind word. I really do not blame them. Most had cigarettes lighted, and no one dared get close to me.

When I finally drove away, I went over a curb, caused an oncoming car to swerve into a ditch, and most disturbingly, forgot to pick up my burgers and tacos.

Mom was frantic when the brand new car and I limped into the driveway. She was so excited I was alive (I had been gone for over an hour), she didn't say much about the huge dent in the door, but she said enough: "You'll have to deal with your father when he gets home on Friday."

Alas! Friday came right on schedule. I was in the den, awaiting the inevitable. Around three o'clock I heard Dad drive up in the driveway. He parked the old car right next to the brand new car—you remember, the one with the big dent in the door.

Dad walked through the front door. His footsteps got louder and louder. Sweat began pouring down my face. For a brief moment, I thought I was in a Hitchcock movie.

Dad spotted me in the den. Our eyes locked. Finally, Dad spoke. I remember the entire conversation word for word.

"David, what happened to the car?"

"I took the car to the Jack-in-the-Box, it ran out of gas, a very nice lady gave me a push from behind, she pushed a little too hard, pushed me into a pole, and that's the truth."

"David, were you hurt?"

"No, sir. No one was hurt."

"That's good. I am sure glad you were not hurt. And David, don't worry about the car. That's why we have insurance."

He turned and walked into his room. Not a word of condemnation. No punishment. I was not even grounded for a day, much less the month I was expecting. Not a word was ever said again about the dumb fifteen-year-old and the Jack-in-the-Box.

Years later I heard a story about an adulterous woman and Jesus and how he looked at her and said those immortal words: "Then neither do I condemn you" (John 8:11 NIV).

And I think I understood.

Now you know why my daddy was and still is, my hero. And you know why I cannot throw out that old hat.

In 2004, we took our oldest son, Adam, out to eat lunch on his wedding day. We had searched and searched for the perfect gift for him—something sentimental. Nothing seemed right. On the day we left for his wedding, I found the old golf hat, and the search ended. As I gave it to him, I told him how much I wished my dad could have seen this day and that the hat would always remind him of a kind, gentle, forgiving man he called Paw-Paw, who was still teaching us about the goodness of our other Father.

Cleaning out the closet can indeed be profound.

Benny Goodman and the Raised Eyebrow

Honey, you remember that song?

—Valerie Young Mathews

Prayer confuses me. That should surprise no one who knows me. As noted earlier, I hear that some people praise God for giving them a parking spot closer to the front of Wal-Mart because they prayed. That bothers me just a bit when others beg and beg God to heal their baby of a disease, yet the baby dies anyway. A parking spot a few feet closer matters to God, but an innocent baby's health does not?

I do know and believe that God's wisdom reigns, not mine. In fact, my wisdom is really foolishness compared to God's. I honestly believe that. I just do not buy into the theory that God gave someone a good parking spot. Of course, one argues, God can do whatever he desires, and perhaps he had a good reason for the parking spot response. Yes, all true, but I still don't really believe prime parking is on his to-do list very often.

Sue just left my office. At least half the brand new tissue box is now empty. She and her husband have four children, plus one, now minus one. Almost three years ago, Corrie was born to a couple that had immense problems. Sue and Bob heard about their struggles and offered to help. So they began to care for Corrie and keep her when her parents could not, which amounted to the vast majority of the time.

The day came when the Department of Human Services came in and took Corrie from her drug-induced, homeless parents, and temporary custody was rightfully awarded to Sue and Bob. For over two years Corrie was "theirs." Last week the judge decided that Corrie, now three, should go live with another couple, because that couple had custody of Corrie's half-sister. That explains why the box of tissues in my office is half gone this afternoon. Alas, the day is not over as yet. By the time I leave for home in a couple of hours, the tissues might be all gone, and I am the only one in the office. I will never forget Sue's words.

> I prayed a thousand prayers that God would give Corrie to the family that could help her the most. I knew we were the best family for her. They have never known her or even seen her. We are the only parents she has had. She calls me Mommy and Bob, Daddy. She screamed when they took her. I just don't get this. Why did God choose them? My only conclusion is that I did something wrong. I was not good enough.

And the box of tissues continued to shrink.

My view of prayer, by necessity, and my view of God have drastically changed over the years. Though God cannot make sense to this flawed human brain all the time, he must make sense some of the time.

"Sue," I began, "you might not agree with what I am about to say, but I beg you to think about it. I do not believe for a moment that God made this decision. I am not saying the decision is wrong, but it certainly could be. In fact, I believe it *was* wrong. You and Bob have been wonderful parents to Corrie."

I continued to explain my "logic." The decision was made by one single human being with a mind of his/her own. Our prayer had been for months that Sue and Bob would be chosen as her parents. But how does one called God go about forcing humans to make the *right* decision? If God made our decisions for us, well then we would not be *us,* we would be *robot-us* at best. And there would never be a wrong decision. No real choices; no choices to sin or to obey God. No choice to love; no emotion at all. Just robot-like creatures doing the right thing because a power bigger than we made all the right decisions *for* us. So, in effect, no *us.*

So should we pray? Of course. God has ways to nudge us, to open doors for us, to close other doors, to lead people to us, to counsel us, to guide us through whatever means he chooses. As I have said often, if God could talk to a man through a donkey, I believe God can do other things I would not have considered. But this I do know: whatever God does in helping us make the right decisions, he does so in the context of our free will. I have the free will to walk through those doors God has opened or to ignore them. God, said Paul, will not allow us to be tempted in such a way that we must choose sin. Paul argued that with any temptation comes a way for me to say no. (See 1 Corinthians 10:13.)

My father began the Alzheimer's symptoms in his early seventies. As the disease progressed, Mom resolutely cared for him. Nothing any of her children said could convince her to put Dad in the dreaded nursing home.

We had moved to Michigan about 1200 miles away from Houston. As Dad slipped farther and farther away from reality, my prayers changed, from "Please heal him physically" to "Please take him home quickly." As the months passed and Dad still lived, my anger at God grew. "Why, God? Why don't you just take him?" I was asking respectfully. "Just take him home, before Mom has to change his diapers."

As many can relate, I felt helpless. Living so far away, I couldn't just go visit regularly. As every Sunday came and I climbed into that pulpit to preach about the love of God, I quite frankly felt totally hypocritical, for at times I doubted the very thing I was preaching.

Alas, the day came when the dam broke. My sister had gone for a visit and reported tearfully that Mom had indeed begun to change Dad's diaper.

"I just don't get it, Ann," I began. "Every Sunday, I preach on how much God loves us, yet he refuses to take Dad home. I specifically asked him to take Dad before he was totally humiliated. There is no good reason to prolong this. I seriously doubt if God is even hearing anything I am saying to him. I don't know if I can preach one more sermon – ever."

During that time I had remembered a teacher who taught down the hall from me. She was one of those heroes of the faith, in her seventies when I knew her. One day, she wasn't looking so good. I asked her what was wrong. She was obviously angry, which was highly unusual for her.

"It's my mother. She has bone cancer and is in tremendous pain. This has been going on for months. She's ninety-four years old, and this is getting ridiculous. I thought my faith was so strong, but now I have no idea if God ever hears me. I simply cannot fathom why he doesn't have mercy on her and take her."

After hearing my threat to quit preaching, my sister began to tell me of her recent visit. She called it one of the highlights of her life. "But I thought you told me Mom has to change Dad's diapers."

"She does, but it's the most wonderful thing to see Mom love Dad so much. She has taught me what love is all about. I don't think I have ever seen such devoted love."

A few days later, it was my turn. We were told Dad could die at any moment. So I flew to Houston to be with him one more time.

As the week progressed, Dad never acknowledged my presence. He never opened his eyes. I helped Mom shave him, feed him, and yes, change his diapers. At least, I thought, he has no idea his youngest son is doing this unthinkable, humiliating act.

It was a Thursday, my last day to be with him. Mom and I were spoon-feeding Dad a milkshake. The radio was on in their bedroom where Dad was on his hospital bed. The station was set, not on an oldies station but on an ancient one, playing hits from the '30s and '40s. A Benny Goodman song was playing.

"I know it's silly, but I think he likes the music. It was the music of our sparkin' years." Evidently even people from New Zealand knew what sparkin' was.

Mom and Dad had met during World War II. Dad was stationed in New Zealand, and the sparkin' began in earnest in 1943.

As Mom was wiping Dad's forehead with a wet cloth, she suddenly gasped. "What is it, Mom?" I asked. "That song—that's *our* song, the song we first danced to on our first date."

Mom began to cry, as did her youngest child. She looked at Dad and gently and lovingly said, "Do you remember that song, honey? We must have danced a hundred dances to that one."

Suddenly, the earth moved and angels sang. Dad, who had not responded in a week or shown any life at all, raised his right eyebrow and managed a smile, telling his bride that he indeed remembered Benny Goodman and that song. And the angels sang a bit louder.

I never saw Dad alive again after that day. He died a week later. I now know he died at just the right time. Had he died when I wanted, I would have missed the answer to the prayers I had cried out to God during their hate-filled years. "Please, God, please let my mom and dad love each other again."

Had I been in charge, I would have cut short that love which was rekindled the day Mom kissed Dad. I would have never seen a devoted wife love the way God loves us. I would have missed the raised eyebrow. And that would have been a very sad thing.

It Is Finished

"If they are quiet, the rocks will cry out."

Luke 24 (NIV)

One day, Jesus acted out of character—he decided to plan his own party where he would be the guest of honor. "Go get two donkeys, and let's get this party going," he told his stunned friends.

Now that was a bit confusing to them... and to me. The Jesus I know would never do that. He spent his life thinking of others and always giving his Father the credit for everything. Why such a change?

Apparently his friends knew that when Jesus said to do something, he had good reasons. So they dutifully went and secured the two donkeys, and the party indeed commenced.

As Jesus made his way into the holy city on that donkey, the crowd began to emerge. A few weeks ago when I was in Nashville, a mob of young people had crowded the street I was on, and the police were re-directing the traffic. As we were stopped, I asked an officer what the commotion was all about. The kids seemed giddy and a little out of control and there were thousands of them.

"Oh, it's Justin Bieber. He is filming a music video."

Of course, I had never heard of Justin Bieber. I seem to know him a lot better now.

I imagine the party for Jesus was similar, except the revelers were adults, and the Man who excited them was riding a donkey. I suppose there were some visitors in the city that day that did not know what was happening. Can you hear them asking someone, "What's all the commotion about?"

"Oh," someone might have replied, "it's a man called Jesus—he is our new King!"

So the celebration continued, and the strange thing is that Jesus accepted the praise.

"Teacher, control your followers. They are much too loud. They are giving praise to the wrong king. Tell them to be quiet. This could get us and you in a lot of trouble."

I can almost hear Jesus say something like this: "Terribly sorry for the trouble, but you simply don't understand the significance of what's happening. You see, if these people were quiet, well, how shall I say this? If they were quiet, these rocks here by the side of the road would cry out just as loud. Nothing is going to stop this celebration!"

And the question I have yet again for this incredible Jesus centers on why? Why are the people celebrating, and why are the rocks excited also?

Earlier in this book I presented some stern questions for God. I stated that my main question for God is not now, "Do you exist?" My question for God is, "Where are you when the innocents are being slaughtered?" I now am convinced he has answered the question. He is standing right beside all the innocents. He has heard all their cries. He has dealt with the problem.

Jesus planned his own party because the party is really for us—for all those who are hurting and confused and asking those tough questions. He entered that holy city full of hurting people, and victory over all their hurts, sins, and death issues was merely hours away. He was about to win the game, and the recipients of the championship trophy were and are anyone who will accept it. Death and sin are about to be defeated. And this old world will forever be changed.

Hanging on a cross must be tougher than anything imaginable. I do not know the numbers who have experienced it. I do know this: only One has hung on a cross with the weight of each of our sins forcing the spikes deeper.

The cries he uttered from that cross are recorded for us all. We know what the dying Savior said before he breathed his last. What a blessing, if we will only pause long enough and drink deeply of those words.

I do believe each of the sayings is worthy of a book. I end this book with his last saying. It really says it all: "It is Finished!"

One more question for you, Jesus: *what* is finished?

Jesus's answer is simple, and indeed hopeful. "He is saying that all of it is finished. All the pain, and hurts, and abuse, and hunger. All the sins we struggle with, others' and ours. All the tragedies and the unfairness of life. All of it. It is *all* finished.

And scripture states that Jesus said that *in a loud voice*. I do believe he wanted us all to hear it down through the ages.

It is the kiss for which we have all longed.

It is finished!

About the Author

David and his wife Debbie have been married since 1974. They have four married children, and four granddaughters.

He graduated from Harding University and Harding University Graduate School in Memphis with degrees in Bible, and Philosophy of Religion. He also has a Master's Degree in Substance Abuse Counseling from the University of Louisiana in Monroe.

In 2008, David and Debbie cofounded the Spark of Life Foundation (www.sparkoflife.org), which offers, free of charge, Grief Recovery Retreats for those who have experienced loss. Both David and Debbie are Certified Specialists in Grief Recovery. David is the Executive Director of the foundation.

David and Debbie also conduct Grief Workshops for churches and other organizations around the country. David also is available to conduct "Guilt of God?" workshops for churches. Contact him at david@sparkoflife.org

CROSS-PROMOTIONAL AD FOR SPARK OF LIFE

SPARK OF LIFE GRIEF RECOVERY RETREATS

The Spark of Life Foundation offers 3-day retreats in a resort setting that focus on helping grievers cope with loss. Spark of Life Retreats are funded by private donations and are offered free of charge to those who have experienced loss. All rooms, food, and materials are provided at no cost to any participant. Transportation to the retreat is not provided.

Each retreat is open to any adult who has experienced devastating loss, along with any family member or supportive friend. Teenagers are also welcome who attend with a parent or guardian. The retreats are not associated with any religious group. People from all walks of life are welcome.

Spark of Life Grief Recovery Retreats are led by David and Debbie Mathews, Rusty and Nancy Meadows, and Dennis and Terri Rine, each of whom are certified specialists in grief recovery.

Each retreat is characterized by acceptance, understanding and hope. The retreats have dynamic group interaction and a proven action plan for grief recovery that inspires hope.

SPARK OF LIFE FOUNDATION

The Spark of Life Foundation exists to instill hope, that though life can never be the same after loss, life can still be rich and fulfilling. The founders of Spark of Life have experienced the journey from loss to life, from grief to hope. We know the journey is difficult, but possible. We invite you to join us on this journey to help those who are grieving. The Spark of Life Foundation is a non-profit, 501(c)3 organization. For more information, to register for a retreat, or to make a donation, go to www.sparkoflife.org.

Endnotes

1. Lewis, C.S. *Out of the Silent Planet.* (HarperCollins: New York, NY 2005).
2. Plantinga, Alvin, ed., *The Ontological Argument* (Doubleday Anchor: New York, NY 1965), p. 5.
3. Ibid, p. ix.
4. Hick, John. *The Existence of God* (MacMillan 1976), p. 169.
5. Plantinga, op cit., p. 5.
6. Lewis, C.S. *God in the Dock* (Wm. B. Eerdmans 1972), pp. 52–53.
7. Tozer, A. W. *The Pursuit of God.* (Christian Publications, Inc.: Camp Hill, PA 1982), p. 6.
8. Ibid, p. 16.
9. Ibid, p. 10.
10. Tozer, A. W. *The Pursuit of God.* (Christian Publications, Inc.: Camp Hill, PA 1982), p. 10.
11. Lewis, C. S., *Mere Christianity.* (Broadman & Holman: Nashville, TN 1999).

12. Caputo, Michael, *God–Seen Through the eyes of the Greatest Minds.* (Howard Publishing: West Monroe, LA 2000), p. 45

13. Lewis, C.S., op. cit.

14. Bonhoeffer, Dietrich, A Year with Dietrich Bonhoeffer: Daily Meditations from His Letters, Writings, and Sermons. (Harper One: New York, NY 2005).

15. Lemmons, Albert. Private correspondence, used by permission.

16. Ibid.